WRITERS AND THEIR WORK

ISOBEL ARMSTRONG
General Editor

STEPHEN CRANE

STEPHEN CRANE

From a portrait in oil of Stephen Crane aged 22 in 1894, by Corwin Knapp Linson. Reproduced by courtesy of the Clifton Waller Barrett Library, University of Virginia Library.

STEPHEN CRANE

Kevin J. Hayes

NORTHCOTE

BRITISH COUNCIL

ATLANTIC
PUBLISHERS & DISTRIBUTORS (P) LTD

This edition is published by

ATLANTIC

PUBLISHERS & DISTRIBUTORS (P) LTD

7/22, Ansari Road, Darya Ganj, New Delhi-110 002
Tel: 40775252, 23273880, 23275880, 23280451; Fax: +91-11-23285873
E-mail: orders@atlanticbooks.com; Web: www.atlanticbooks.com

By arrangement with
Northcote House Publishers Ltd
Horndon House, Horndon, Tavistock, Devon, PL19 9NQ,
United Kingdom. (T)+44(0)1822 810066; (F)+44(0)1822 810034
(E) northcote.house@virgin.net and (W) www.northcotehouse.co.uk
The *Writers and their Work* series is published in association with the British Council.

First Indian Reprint 2010
First published in 2004 by Northcote House Publishers Ltd

ISBN 978-81-269-1313-8

For Sale in the Indian sub-continent only. Not for export elsewhere.

British Library Cataloguing-in-Publication Data
A catalogue record for this book is available from the British Library

Typeset by TW Typesetting, Plymouth, Devon
Printed in India at Nice Printing Press, A-33/3A, Site-IV,
Industrial Area, Sahibabad, Ghaziabad, U.P.

To Myung-Sook

Contents

Biographical Outline

1871 1 November, Stephen Crane born at Newark, New Jersey, the fourteenth and last child of the Revd Dr Jonathan Townley Crane and Mary Helen Peck.

1876 The Crane family moves to Paterson, New Jersey. Stephen receives primary education from his sister Agnes Elizabeth.

1878 Dr Crane becomes pastor of Drew Methodist Church in Port Jervis, New York. Stephen enrolls in public school.

1880 On 16 February, Crane's father dies.

1883 Townley Crane, an older brother, begins operating a summer news agency in the resort town of Asbury Park, New Jersey. Mrs Crane moves her family there in June.

1885 Crane enrolls in the Pennington Seminary in Pennington, New Jersey.

1887 Crane abruptly leaves Pennington Seminary near the year's end.

1888 In January Crane registers at Claverack College and Hudson River Institute, a military school, as a student in the Classical Department, but later transfers to the Academic Department. In July he begins assisting his brother Townley with his Asbury news-reporting agency. He returns each summer through 1892 in a similar capacity.

1890 Crane enrolls as a freshman in the mining-engineering programme at Lafayette College, Easton, Pennsylvania.

1891 Crane transfers to the University of Syracuse in January. He publishes sketches in the *University Herald,* works as stringer for the *New York Tribune,* and plays baseball. He also begins writing an early version of *Maggie* in the Delta Upsilon House. In June he joins friends on a camping trip in Sullivan County, an excursion which would form the basis for his Sullivan County sketches in the *New York Tribune* the following year. In August Hamlin Garland lectures on American literature and art at Avon-by-the-Sea, New Jersey, where he and Crane meet. Late this year Crane begins exploring the tenement districts of New York's Lower East Side.

1892 Jacob A. Riis lectures at Avon-by-the-Sea in July, which Crane reports for the *New York Tribune.* Hamlin Garland returns to Asbury Park, and he and Crane play baseball and discuss literature. Crane moves to New York City in October, sharing a rooming house with several medical students.

1893 In late February or early March *Maggie: A Girl of the Streets* appears. In or around October Crane moves into the old Art Students' League building at 143–147 East 23rd St.

1894 In December an abridged version of *The Red Badge of Courage* appears in syndicated form in the *Philadelphia Press,* the *New York Press,* and several others newspapers across the country.

1895 Crane leaves New York in January for an extensive tour of the West and Mexico to write feature articles for the Bacheller syndicate. In May Copeland and Day publish his first collection of verse, *The Black Riders, and Other Lines.* Appleton publishes *The Red Badge of Courage* in September to instant acclaim.

1896 *George's Mother* appears in May, and the following month Appleton publishes an expurgated edition of *Maggie.* In September Heinemann publishes the first British edition of *Maggie,* prefaced with 'An Appreciation' by William Dean Howells. *The Little Regiment and Other Episodes of the American Civil War* appears in

November. Late that month Crane leaves New York for Jacksonville, Florida, where he meets Cora Taylor.

1897 In January the *Commodore*, sailing from Jacksonville toward Cuba, sinks. Crane escapes in a lifeboat, an experience which leads to his fine short story 'The Open Boat'. He returns to New York and signs a contract with William Randolph Hearst's *New York Journal* to report the impending Graeco-Turkish War. He and Cora travel to Europe, arriving in London in late March and Athens in April. *The Third Violet* appears in May. They settle at Ravensbrook, a small villa in Surrey, where their neighbours include several prominent men of letters.

1898 In February the *USS Maine* is exploded in Havana harbour, killing over two hundred crew members, prompting the US Congress to authorize the use of armed forces to end the civil war in Cuba. Spain and the United States officially declare war on one another. *The Open Boat and Other Tales of Adventure* appears in April. Commissioned as war correspondent for Joseph Pulitzer's *New York World*, Crane makes several brief voyages from Key West to gather information about naval operations with other correspondents, including Frank Norris. In late July Crane briefly returns to New York, breaks with Pulitzer, and signs with Hearst's *New York Journal* to report the Puerto Rican campaign. The following month Crane returns to Cuba and enters Havana illegally. After hostilities end, he remains in Havana for several months, living in virtual seclusion. Cora, still in England, attempts to contact him but is unsuccessful. Before the year's end, Crane leaves Havana for New York and then leaves for England shortly after arriving in New York.

1899 In February Stephen and Cora Crane move into Brede Place. *War Is Kind*, his second collection of verse, appears in May. *Active Service* and *The Monster and Other Stories* are published. 'The Ghost', a dramatic performance largely written by Crane, is performed during the Christmas festivities.

1900 Crane suffers two massive tubercular haemorrhages in April, prompting Cora to raise funds to seek a cure in Badenweiler, Germany. On 5 June he dies in Badenweiler. Several of his works appear posthumously.

Abbreviations and References

C	*The Correspondence of Stephen Crane*, ed. Stanley Wertheim and Paul Sorrentino, 2 vols. (New York:Columbia University Press, 1988)
CH	*Stephen Crane: The Critical Heritage*, ed. Richard M. Weatherford (London: Routledge and Kegan Paul, 1973)
M	*Maggie: A Girl of the Streets (A Story of New York)*, ed. Kevin J. Hayes (Boston: Bedford/St Martin's, 1999)
RB	*The Red Badge of Courage: An Episode of the American Civil War*, ed. Henry Binder (1982; repr. New York: Norton, 1999)
W	*The University of Virginia Edition of the Works of Stephen Crane*, ed. Fredson Bowers, 10 vols. (Charlottesville: University Press of Virginia, 1969–1976)
Work	*The Work of Stephen Crane*, ed. Wilson Follett, 12 vols. (New York: Knopf, 1925)

Introduction

1871, the year of Stephen Crane's birth, marked the centenary of Sir Walter Scott's, which New Yorkers commemorated by erecting a statue of him in Central Park. The enduring respect for Scott's Waverley novels represented by this statue also indicates the ongoing popularity of historical romance among American readers and suggests the difficulty of acceptance Crane and his fellow realist and naturalist authors faced during the final third of the nineteenth century. For the generation of authors who came to prominence after the Civil War, historical romance was something to repudiate. William Dean Howells, the most vocal proponent of realism among American authors, eschewed romance and championed realism both by example – writing realist novels – and by defining its principles in his voluminous critical writings. In France, Émile Zola was giving naturalism its start. Both the realists and the naturalists sought to write realistically, yet they differed in terms of their philosophical outlook. Howells and his followers retained hope and optimism whereas the naturalist writers depicted reality from a deterministic and, therefore, largely pessimistic perspective. In his boyhood Crane read the works of Scott and James Fenimore Cooper – the American Scott, as he was known – yet he, too, came to resent the kind of literature they wrote. Instead, Crane sought a literary style all his own, one that combined elements of realism and naturalism yet also incorporated unique visual imagery and made extensive use of a subjective and often variable point of view.

Crane was born on the first of November – All Saints' Day – in Newark, New Jersey, the son of the Revd Dr Jonathan Townley Crane, presiding elder of the Methodist churches in the Newark district, and Mary Helen Peck. Fundamental differences between the orthodoxy and Dr Crane's unique brand of Methodism prompted his removal from this prestigious position and eventually relegated him to serving as pastor at Drew Methodist Church in Port Jervis, New York, by the late 1870s. After her husband's death in 1880, Mrs Crane stayed put a few more years, and Port Jervis would remain important to Stephen's life and imagination. It provided the model for Whilomville, the small fictional city where he would set his short-story cycle *Whilomville Stories* and a novella, *The Monster*. Port Jervis was also a jumping-off point for holiday visitors to the adjacent Sullivan County, a place which inspired Crane's first important series of imaginative newspaper articles and provided the setting for the first part of his fourth novel, *The Third Violet*. Before Stephen reached his teens, Mrs Crane moved the family to the resort city of Asbury Park, New Jersey, a location she may have chosen because her son Townley was operating a summer news agency there. William Crane, an older brother, remained in Port Jervis and later helped to establish Hartwood, a fine hunting lodge in Sullivan County. Both William's home and his hunting lodge frequently lured Stephen back to the area.

Crane continued restless through his late teens. He spent summers working for Townley's news agency and during the school year attended a series of high schools and colleges, never staying for very long at any of them. After spending the spring term of 1891 at Syracuse University, he decided not to return in September, at which time he initiated a programme of self-education by exploring the tenement districts of New York's Lower East Side. The experience would prove invaluable for his first novel, *Maggie: A Girl of the Streets*, a work he began drafting while at Syracuse and continued tinkering with into 1892. Unable to find a publisher for the novel he exhausted a modest legacy to publish the book himself. *Maggie* appeared in early 1893 but was largely ignored.

Crane moved into the old Art Students' League building on East 23rd St in 1893. Living amidst several artists, he obtained material inspiring some early sketches and the later portion of *The Third Violet*. Furthermore, life among artists allowed him the opportunity to develop his visual aesthetic. Here he wrote

The Red Badge of Courage. Lauded for its innovative visual imagery, *Red Badge*, it should not be forgotten, was written among artists. Crane initially had difficulty placing this novel with a publisher, until Irving Bacheller accepted a greatly abbreviated version for his newspaper syndicate. Published in newspapers across the nation, *Red Badge* firmly established Crane's reputation. Appleton, a prominent New York publisher, expressed interest in the work and eventually accepted it.

1895 was a watershed year for Crane. The success of *Red Badge* in syndicated form prompted Bacheller to hire Crane for an extensive tour of the West and Mexico to write feature articles for his newspaper syndicate. The trip resulted in a series of sketches of uneven quality yet ultimately provided experiences that inspired some of Crane's finest short stories. Copeland and Day, a Boston firm, published his first volume of poetry, *The Black Riders, and Other Lines*, in May, and Appleton published *Red Badge* in late September. Reviews of Crane's poetry were mixed, but the novel received warm and enthusiastic praise. It has remained in print ever since.

Given the critical and financial success of *Red Badge*, Appleton became anxious to publish other Crane novels. He offered the publisher *Maggie* and another slum novel, *George's Mother*, which he had written shortly after completing *Maggie*. Appleton published both in 1896, though *Maggie* appeared in expurgated form. Many contemporary readers saw them as aberrations that took Crane away from his true calling as an author of war stories. His reputation as the author of *Red Badge* prompted attention from magazine editors who were anxious for other tales of the Civil War. He obliged, and several magazine pieces appeared in 1896. He collected six of them as *The Little Regiment and Other Episodes of the American Civil War*, which was published by the year's end. *The Little Regiment* affirmed Crane's reputation as an author of war stories. British readers, especially, received the book with fondness. The London *Echo* (27 February 1897), for example, called Crane 'the first author to describe war as it really is' and found that he 'seized upon an aspect of it that has never been treated before, by painter or writer. He shows us its utter commonplaceness, apart from its accompaniments of maiming and killing. Many a youth has taken the Queen's shilling, or run off to sea, under the spell of a fighting novel. But no story of Mr Crane's will have that effect. War as he paints it, is too vulgar, unheroic a business to turn any youngster's brain.'

Crane's interests turned him toward Cuba, where he hoped to cover the Cuban revolution. His repeated attempts to reach Cuba from Jacksonville, Florida, were thwarted, however. During his stay in Jacksonville he met Cora Taylor, who was operating a house of assignation known as the Hotel de Dream. They became a couple, and before long Cora was calling herself Mrs Stephen Crane, though they were never officially married. In a further attempt to reach Cuba, Crane sailed aboard the *Commodore*, which foundered and sank. He escaped in an open boat, an experience which gave rise to one of his finest short stories.

Opportunities as a war correspondent fed Crane's restlessness. Newspaperman Robert H. Davis, conveying the difficulty he had locating him around this time, observed, 'Crane possessed not only a magic quill but one perfectly good pair of seven-league boots as well. He seemed ill disposed to remain in any one place long enough to be located' (*Work*, ii. xi–xii). In March 1897 Crane returned to New York and signed a contract with William Randolph Hearst's *New York Journal* to report the impending Greco-Turkish War. He and Cora travelled to Europe together, arriving in Athens in April, the month Turkey declared war on Greece.

Crane spent the last few years of his all too brief life either in war or around books. After the Graeco-Turkish War had ended, he and Cora settled at Ravensbrook, a small villa in Surrey, where their neighbours included several prominent men of letters: Robert Barr, Joseph Conrad, Harold Frederic, Edward Garnett, Ford Madox Hueffer (later known as Ford Madox Ford), and Henry James. The experience was a rich one and gave Crane a group of like-minded souls, friends who appreciated and encouraged his work. At the time he was constantly in need of money and wrote as fast and as much as he possibly could. Having settled in England, Crane would seem headed for a period of relative stability, but the Spanish–American War ended that.

In April 1898, Spain and the United Stated declared war on one another, and the following month Crane was commissioned as war correspondent for Joseph Pulitzer's *New York World*. His war dispatches, many written close to the fighting, furthered his reputation as a keen observer of combat. Switching from Pulitzer's *World* to Hearst's *New York Journal*, Crane next reported the Puerto Rican campaign and then spent some months in Havana. February found him back in England, where he and Cora moved into Brede Place, a dilapidated, centuries-old country place. The damp, drafty old pile lured numerous houseguests, yet its upkeep compelled Crane to write at a furious pace. Regardless of its charm, Brede Place must have been one of the worst possible places for a consumptive to live. In April 1900 Crane suffered two massive tubercular haemorrhages. Cora raised funds to seek a cure for him at a sanatorium in Badenweiler, Germany, but by the time they reached Germany Crane was long past being cured. He died on 5 June 1900. He was 28.

A series of factors have adversely shaped the course of Stephen Crane's critical reputation: the squeamishness of his contemporary editors, the charlatanism of his first biographer, and the tunnel vision of academics who have explicated his work without regard to important evidence.

Though Appleton agreed to publish *The Red Badge of Courage*, its editors insisted that Crane alter his text to soften the novel's ironic depiction of war. The Appleton text established Crane's reputation as an author, but it also presented readers with much ambiguity that had not been a part of *Red Badge* as Crane had originally completed it. The Appleton *Maggie* differed significantly from the first edition Crane had published himself. Much vulgar language and graphic description was excised from the novel. The original manuscript of *Red Badge* and multiple copies of the first edition of *Maggie* have survived, but they were ignored for several decades.

In terms of the critical and biographical studies that followed Crane's death, none was more instrumental in establishing his lasting reputation than Henry Beer's *Stephen Crane*. Beer gave readers a personable and adventuresome Crane who lived the life of the stories he told. There is only one problem: Beer's biography was a near-complete fabrication. His general way of working was to take a Crane story he liked, identify a prominent motif from it, and then invent an episode in Crane's life that anticipated the story. Beer falsified the story of Crane's life in other ways. He fabricated letters and attributed them to Crane and made up letters from Crane's correspondents, too. Beer's lies went undetected for decades, and the words he put in Crane's mouth were quoted time and again in the critical literature.

The major reason why the flaws in Crane's texts and biography went unnoticed for so long was because structuralism, the prevailing form of academic criticism of the twentieth century, placed no emphasis on textual or biographical research. In the United States, this critical approach became known as the New Criticism, and the New Critics deliberately analysed the formal elements of a literary work without regard to its history.

It was not until the 1970s and 1980s that the problematic nature of Crane's texts and biography became recognized. The new discoveries that have been made in recent decades have rendered much that has been said about Crane irrelevant. Though it is regrettable that so many critical studies are now obsolete, it is exciting to realize that Crane's life and works must be studied afresh. Much work remains to be done.

The present study is one of a few book-length works devoted to the task of re-evaluating Crane's oeuvre in light of the new evidence that has emerged in recent decades. In addition, this work takes advantage of new trends in critical thinking. Specifically, it situates Crane's works within a matrix of competing cultural contexts. Crane's novels, short stories, and poetry owe a debt to folk culture, especially folk speech, legend, and the tall tale. Furthermore, Crane's writings have an ambivalent relationship with late-nineteenth-century popular culture. They frequently criticize the easy sentimentalism of stage melodrama and dime novels but do not mask the influence of popular culture. In addition, Crane's unique visual sensibilities attuned him to the increasing importance of popular visual culture in the late nineteenth century.

Arrange in chronological order, the following chapters trance Crane's writings from his early newspaper work through to his last great novella. Chapter 1, 'Sullivan County Sketches', shows how Crane's series of newspaper articles make use of traditional materials and tests our ideas and narrative strategies he would develop in his greatest works. Chapter 2, 'Maggie's World', analyses Crane's first novel and takes a sidelong glance at his third, *George's Mother*. Both are urban slum novels, and both show how the mean streets of Manhattan influence the lives of the men and women who live there. This chapter also seeks to situate Crane's work within the general contexts of American literary realism and naturalism.

Chapter 3, 'Black Riders', examines the relationship between Crane's poetry and American literary history. His verse recalls the work of the finest American poets before him – Edgar Allan Poe, Walt Whitman, Emily Dickinson – and anticipates the imagists and other modernists to come. In addition, the chapter discusses the relationship of Crane's poetry to the print culture of its day. Chapter 4, 'Image and Emblem in *The Red Badge of Courage*', parallels the visual techniques Crane used in his great war novel with the cinema, which emerged around the same time. What the pioneers of motion pictures were doing on film, Crane was doing with the written word. Chapter 5, 'Love, Art, Work: *The Third Violet*', looks at Crane's neglected fourth novel. Though often labelled a potboiler, *The Third Violet* possesses considerably more sophistication than has been realized. Overall, this novel constitutes an essay on the creative process and its relationship to the marketplace.

Crane's dispatches from Puerto Rico and Cuba during the Spanish–American war have generally received more critical attention that those from the Graeco-Turkish War, but chapter 6, 'War Dispatches', concentrates on those from Greece. Written over a hundred years ago, Crane's commentary on the relationship between Greek and Turk, West and East, Christian and Muslim remains pertinent. Chapter 7, 'Point of View and the Short Story', examines three of Crane's most well-regarded tales – 'A Man and Some Others', 'The Blue Hotel', 'The Open Boat' – to show how shrewdly he manipulated narrative point of view. *The Monster* has been receiving an enormous amount of critical attention lately. Taking a different approach from other recent essays, Chapter 8, '*The Monster*: The Idea of Order at Whilomville', discusses this novella in terms of concepts that have intrigued such modernist and postmodernist authors from Wallace

Stevens to Thomas Pynchon. Finally, the conclusion offers an overview of Crane's literary reputation as it pertains to the history of war.

1

Sullivan County Sketches

Stephen Crane's earliest imaginative work includes a series of newspaper contributions he wrote in the 1890s, which would become known collectively as the Sullivan County sketches. Written in different literary styles and sometimes set at different points in time, these sketches nevertheless share common ground, for all are set in or near Sullivan County, a woodsy area of rural New York bordering on Pennsylvania where Crane sometimes went camping with friends and enjoyed a variety of other outdoor pursuits. Though he would later group eight of these newspaper sketches together for a collection he proposed to Copeland and Day, he did not initially conceive the series as a whole. In the half-hearted proposal, written three years after he had completed the final sketch in the series, Crane provided an indication of how he saw them: 'little grotesque tales of the woods which I wrote when I was clever' (C i. 111). While some of the later Sullivan County sketches have the quality of grotesqueries, not all do. In *Cylinder of Vision: The Fiction and Journalistic Writing of Stephen Crane,* Milne Holton compares the Sullivan County sketches to the short stories that comprise Ernest Hemingway's *In Our Time.*[1] The early writings of each author show him in the process of learning his writerly trade, honing his voice, and developing the unique style his greatest works would fulfil. Though Hemingway's early work has received much critical attention, Crane's Sullivan County sketches possess a complexity that has yet to be fully appreciated. Seemingly light-hearted, they ultimately interrogate the meaning and purpose of narrative.

The first published sketch, 'The Last of the Mohicans', reiterates the title of one of the most highly regarded works in

American literature at the time, yet Crane co-opts James Fenimore Cooper's title, not to pay homage, but rather to take his literary predecessor to task. In its original appearance in the *New York Tribune* (21 February 1892), Crane's sketch is titled 'The Last of the Mohicans: His Aspect in Fiction Contradicted by His Fame in Folklore'. This article anticipates Mark Twain's more familiar essay, 'Fenimore Cooper's Literary Offenses', which would appear three years later. While the literary styles of Crane and Twain differ significantly, both shared a dislike for historical romance and sought grittier ways of writing. Crane had not always held as much animosity toward Cooper as this sketch conveys, however. He was a precocious child and, according to one account, had read Cooper when he was 4 years old (*W* x. 345). Despite his father's disapproval, young Crane also read nickel and dime novels, which helped direct his attention toward a more realistic writing style. While the romantic plots of the dime novels often echoed those of Cooper and his contemporaries, their frequent use of realistic settings and vernacular language helped point the way to literary realism.

'The Last of the Mohicans' contrasts folklore with literary culture and questions the value of the written word in comparison to oral tradition. The sketch begins by suggesting camaraderie between legend and history. Time and again, Crane asserts, 'most of these fireside stories are verified by books written by learned men, who have dived into piles of mouldy documents and dusty chronicles to establish their facts' (*W* viii. 199). The sketch ends with a highfalutin quotation from the mouth of one of Fenimore Cooper's Indians and, for comparison, a realistic physical description of the last Mohican of Sullivan County. Though not necessarily intended as such, 'The Last of the Mohicans' serves as an introduction to the Sullivan County sketches, for it asserts the validity of retelling old legends, which possess a veracity superior to that of the romanticized versions that could be found in the novels of a previous generation. Thematically, 'The Last of the Mohicans' establishes a two-against-one discursive opposition, history and legend joining forces against romance. This antagonistic relationship, though echoed in subsequent sketches, is not fully sustained over their course.

'Hunting Wild Hogs', the second Sullivan County sketch to appear, begins with a reference to legends about hunting panthers in the American wilderness, and follows with a reference to bear hunting, topics subsequent sketches would develop at greater length. 'Mayhap, in a thousand varieties of chimney-corner', Crane observes, 'old, gnarled and knotted forty-niners curdle the blood and raise the hair of their listeners with legends of the ferocious and haughty grizzly bear' (*W* viii. 201). Wild hog hunting is a different story altogether. Since wild hogs are not indigenous to North America and especially not to Sullivan County, the only hogs that could be hunted were those five that had escaped from the country estate of Otto Plank, who had imported them from Europe. Crane, therefore, notes that there were only a few men 'who have proper right to thrill anybody, curdle any blood, or raise any hair with tales of the hunting and killing of the famous wild hogs of ancient and modern Europe upon the territory of the United States' (*W* viii. 201).

Legend is at odds with history in 'Hunting Wild Hogs'. The local panther-hunting and bear-hunting stories may or may not be true. Since both creatures are indigenous to North America, there is no way of quantifying the actual number that may have existed or that may have been tracked and killed. When it comes to wild hogs, however, the animals can be quantified and the number killed, therefore, can be historically verified. According to Sullivan County oral tradition, however, the number of legendary hogs far outstripped the number of actual hogs. 'Children going to school were frightened home by wild hogs', Crane observes. 'Men coming home late at night saw wild hogs. It became a sort of fashion to see wild hogs and turn around and come back' (*W* viii. 202). In other words, the legends could not withstand historical scrutiny. Crane's attitude toward the local legends of wild hog hunting is ultimately ambivalent. While exploding their vulgar errors, he obviously enjoys their verve.

'Not Much of a Hero', published two months after 'Hunting Wild Hogs', tells the story of Tom Quick, whose reputation rests on his legendary exploits as an Indian killer. The sketch initially describes Quick, explains how local people erected a monument to him, and quotes the monument's inscription: 'Tom Quick was the first white child born within the present borough of Milford' (*W* viii. 211). The remainder of the sketch attempts to reconcile Quick's legendary reputation with this matter-of-fact inscription. The discrepancy between legend and fact is, according to Crane, partially due to Quick's literary reputation. Historical romance again plays the villain, for it has interceded between history and legend and turned them into opposites. Tom Quick, Crane asserts, was a boy's hero and had been 'a subject for the graphic and brilliant pens of the talented novelists of the dime and five-cent school. Youths going westward to massacre the devoted red man with a fell purpose and a small-calibre revolver always carry a cheap edition of Tom Quick's alleged biography, which is, when they are at a loss how to proceed, a valuable book of reference' (*W* viii. 212). According to Crane, the published tales of Tom Quick show how one discursive genre could be read as another. In this case, a romanticized biography could function as a how-to manual. Stories of thrilling adventure influenced behaviour and helped justify all sorts of atrocities.

Crane exaggerates the influence of the dime novels on the settling of the American West for his own purposes, however. In relation to the history of westward migration, the nickel and dime novels emerged fairly late. Discussing Tom Quick's literary reputation, Crane may have had in mind R. T. Emmet's *Tom Quick, The Avenger of the Delaware* (1889), published just a few years before as part of the series 'The Five Cent Wide Awake Library'. Locally, the story of Tom Quick had recently been dramatized, and Crane probably knew James M. Allerton's stageplay *Tom Quick, The Avenger; or, One Hundred for One: An Historical Tragedy in Five Acts* (1888), the text of which was published at Port Jervis, New York.

Crane reaches a point in 'Not Much of a Hero' where he contrasts the viewpoints of historian, romanticist, and teller of legends: 'Historians are, as a rule, unsentimental. The aesthetic people, the lovers of the beautiful, the poetic dreamers, have always claimed that Quick during his lifetime killed one hundred Indians. The local historians stoutly assert that he only killed fifteen at most' (*W* viii. 212). These three different approaches lead to three different views of Quick, which Crane summarizes in his conclusion to the sketch: 'The deeds which are accredited to him may be fiction ones and he may have been one of those sturdy and bronzed woodsmen who cleared the path of civilization. Or the accounts may be true and he a monomaniac upon the subject of Indians as suggested by the dramatist. Or the accounts may be true and he a man whose hands were stained with unoffending blood, purely and simply a murderer' (*W* viii. 215).

The first view articulates the attitude of the civic leaders of Milford, the Pennsylvania town just across the border from Sullivan County, as the title of the collection of papers associated with Quick's commemoration clearly shows: *Tom Quick, or The Foundation and the Capstone: Pioneer Enterprise and National Independence*. Crane's specific mention of 'the dramatist' confirms his knowledge of Allerton's play. The third view reflects Crane's own attitude and affirms the title of his sketch. Though exaggerated stories of wild hog hunting gave Crane much pleasure, he could not condone the circulation of stories about Indian killing.

Sketches published shortly after 'Not Much of a Hero' develop the relationships among orally circulated tales and legends, history, and romanticized fiction. In 'Sullivan County Bears', Crane recognizes the difficulty of reconciling 'the bear of fiction with the bear of reality' (*W* viii. 219). In this sketch he mentions the 'black bear of the hunter's tale' and the black bears of the story books, yet he did not explicitly develop the link between the two. In 'The Way in Sullivan County', however, he details the process orally circulated tales underwent as they found their way into print. The sketch begins: 'A country famous for its hunting and its hunters is naturally prolific of liars'. Locals regard one another with suspicion and generally recognize lies when they hear them. The arrival of city folks on holiday, on the other hand, offers the locals a gullible audience who will take their lies as truth. The city man with a penchant for writing listens keenly, 'seizes his pen and with flashing eye and trembling, eager fingers . . . writes those brief but lurid sketches which fascinate and charm the reading public while the virtuous bushwhacker, whittling a stick near by, smiles in his own calm and sweet fashion' (*W* viii. 220–21).

'The Way in Sullivan County' indicates Crane's shrewd understanding of the way tall tales and tall talk worked. Within its social context, the tall tale normally serves to reinforce the identity of a folk group, excluding outsiders and strengthening the bond among insiders. Furthermore, it offers outsiders the opportunity to be initiated into the group. They need only understand the humour of the tall tale, accept it, and go along with whatever lies they are told no matter how outrageous. The outsider who does not recognize the tale's humour or does not appreciate it will remain an outsider. The outsider who transcribes tales from the oral tradition for the purpose of seeing them into print, as the behaviour of the smiling whittler indicates, will remain an outsider and will become an object of humour to the members of the folk group.

Having explored and articulated the various relationships among orally circulated tales and legends, history, and historical romance, Crane tired of the subject and decided to take his series of sketches in a significantly different direction. 'Four Men in a Cave', published the first week of July 1892, marks an extraordinary departure for the Sullivan County sketches, as the two sentences that open the article indicate:

> The moon rested for a moment in the top of a tall pine on a hill. The little man was standing in front of the camp-fire making oration to his companions. (*W* viii. 225)

Gone are references to specific people and locations. In their place appear transcendent visions of the natural world and anonymous figures defined by their physical characteristics. In place of Crane's interrogation of established narrative genres comes a story that, as it develops, takes for its subject the production of narrative.

The purpose of the little man's oration is to persuade his companions to join him on a spelunking expedition. His friends remain unconvinced until he argues, 'We can tell a great tale when we get back to the city, if we investigate this thing' (*W* viii. 225). Narrative provides oration its most convincing argument, and the possibility of generating personal narratives of thrilling adventure convinces the companions to tag along. They soon find themselves inside the cave, where they encounter a crazy old hermit, who swindles the little man in a card game. Back around the campfire at the tale's end, the little man seethes with rage toward the hermit. One companion, the pudgy man, throws the little man's words back in his face: 'Oh well . . . we can tell a great tale when we get back to the city after having investigated this thing' (*W* viii. 230). The little man's capacity for narrative is gone. 'Go to the devil!' are the only words he can muster in response. While the little man's effort to generate a thrilling story of heroic personal adventure is thwarted, Crane fashions an ironic tale from the little man's behaviour, which conveys the impossibility of romantic adventure.

Later Sullivan County sketches follow the trajectory established by 'Four Men in a Cave' as they demonstrate that even though narratives of heroic adventures are no longer possible, ironic tales of bad campouts are. All feature the little man, and most include the pudgy man and the two other unnamed and unidentified companions. 'The Octopush', for example – the title incorporates the slurred speech of the story's drunken wilderness guide – tells how the guide initially places each of the four men on a different tree stump projecting from the swamp. The guide then proceeds to get drunk and ignores their cries for rescue until he is beset by hallucinations and begins to fear for his life as he perceives that the stump on which he is perched has become an 'octopush'. 'The Cry of a Huckleberry Pudding: A Dim Study of Camping Experiences' tells how the little man, having consumed an entire huckleberry pudding, becomes violently ill in the middle of the night. The other men awake to a mysterious and terrifying sound, 'the chant of a phantom force which imagination declares invincible, and awful to the sight' (*W* viii. 256). They writhe in terror, and their discovery that the little man is missing exacerbates their fears, for they assume a mysterious creature has snatched him away. Only when the little man returns and explains that the noise they had heard was him getting sick from the pudding are their fears allayed. They scold him for scaring them, and he berates them for their lack of sympathy.

'The Octopush' and 'The Cry of a Huckleberry Pudding' mark another shift in Crane's thinking. While both are fairly mundane and certainly unheroic stories of camping experiences, they nevertheless convey the power with which the imagination can interpret reality. In both, imagination, combined with paranoia, supplies what modern backwoods adventure lacked; that is, a sense of terror.

'The Mesmeric Mountain' reiterates the power of the imagination for interpreting the environment. As the story goes, the little man separates himself from his companions to follow an unknown path, which he is sure 'leads to something great or something' (*W* viii. 269). He encounters a mountain that seems to possess a life of its own. He feels its eyes staring at him and perceives the mountain start to chase him. Discussing this sketch in *The Literary Tensions in Stephen Crane's Novels and Short Stories*, Chulwon Cho compares the little man's experience to young William Wordsworth's experience in *The Prelude*.[2] The huge cliff Wordsworth confronts in *The Prelude* uprears its head and, like a living thing, seems to follow him. Whereas Wordsworth escapes from the menace in his skiff, Crane's little man climbs wildly as he attempts to scale the mountain, which tries to shrug him off. The little man finally crests its summit, where he swaggers with triumph. The sketch closes with the following one-sentence paragraph: 'The mountain under his feet was motionless' (*W* viii. 271). As a prose stylist Crane was often at his most masterful in his closing sentences. In subsequent writings, he would use other brief yet striking sentences to close stories or, in the case of his novels, to end particularly dramatic chapters.

This closing sentence underscores the story's approach to narrative point of view, an approach Crane would use time and again in his subsequent fiction. Though told in the third person, the sketch is largely focalized from the protagonist's perspective and therefore articulates his interpretation of the environment. The brief closing sentence remains in the third person, yet shifts from the protagonist's perspective to an objective one. The contrast is striking.

The general tenor of 'The Mesmeric Mountain', the last known Sullivan County sketch, shows that Crane was outstretching the boundaries of the newspaper sketch. As he explained in the letter to Copeland and Day after describing eight of his Sullivan country sketches as 'little grotesque tales': 'The trouble is that they only sum 10,000 words and I can make no more' (*C* i. 111). Crane's statement suggests that he had taken the genre of the backcountry sketch about as far as it could be taken. Though he would continually return to the sketch form – Edwin Cady has gone so far as to suggest that the sketch was Crane's métier and that his novels were largely 'montages of sketches' (*W* viii. xxiii) – this statement to Copeland and Day, read in light of 'The Mesmeric Mountain', suggests that Crane was looking for new ways to articulate his ideas. The motif of a little man confronting the environment he soon found appropriate for verse, and the idea of the personal and idiosyncratic interpretation of the environment would become an important theme of his fiction, in which he would continue to scrutinize the significance of narrative and its influence on behaviour.

2

Maggie's World

Whether he was writing about the backwoods of upstate New York or the back alleys of lower Manhattan, Stephen Crane emphasized the interrelationship between the environment and the individual. Like holiday campers in Sullivan County, urban tenement dwellers interpret the surrounding environment from their personal points of view. Unlike Sullivan County tourists, the urban poor cannot simply leave if the environment becomes frightening or intimidating. They were born there, and there they will die. Like it or not, they are a part of their environment, which has helped to shape who they are. The theme of the urban environment's influence on behaviour pervades Crane's New York stories and is especially apparent in his first novel and most important piece of urban fiction, *Maggie: A Girl of the Streets (A Story of New York).*

Inscribing copies of *Maggie* for friends and well-wishers, Crane made this influence of environment explicit. Several surviving presentation copies of the first edition contain the following statement in Crane's hand: 'It is inevitable that you be greatly shocked by this book but continue, please with all possible courage to the end. For it tries to show that environment is a tremendous thing in the world and frequently shapes lives regardless' (*M* 3). Crane ends the sentence here, but, to extend it, he might have said regardless of any other factors: heredity, personal will, philanthropic aid, anything.

The idea that environment significantly shaped human behaviour was becoming increasingly accepted in Crane's time. Many discussions of New York tenement life published in the leading journals during the half-dozen years before *Maggie* emphasized how growing up in the tenements adversely shaped a person's thought, beliefs, and behaviour. The prevailing attitudes toward the influence of environment were mostly derived from British philosopher Herbert Spencer, who, though largely ignored now, was considered by many contemporaries to be the nineteenth century's most important thinker after Charles Darwin. Spencer theorized that individual organic units joined and acted together as one organism. Over the course of his ambitious career, he applied the idea to many fields of study. Spencer argued that people adapted themselves to their environment by submitting to the will of the social organism to which they belonged. Others applied Spencer's basic theory to moral issues. The Reverend James Huntington, for example, argued that the tenement house environment contributed to the moral decay of its inhabitants. Though Huntington does not mention Spencer, his language clearly reflects Spencer's thinking. Discussing the variety of ethnic groups represented and languages spoken in the tenements, Huntington characterized the tenement dwellers collectively as 'a restless, seething mass of human beings, unable to talk together, unable to think together, able only, under some overmastering passion, to act together' (*M* 123).

As Crane's novel begins, Maggie and Jimmie, her slightly older brother, are slum-dwelling children who must cope with the wrath of Mary Johnson, their drunken, ornery mother, whose main activities seem to be cursing, breaking furniture, and abusing her children. The third chapter, the last depicting their childhood, ends by showing the tremendous fear in which the children live. They enter the flat, find their drunken mother passed out on the floor, become afraid she might wake up and take out her wrath on them, and consequently seek a safe hiding place. The picture of the two children cowering in a dark corner until daybreak offers a striking image of a disturbing, miserable childhood. The squalid environment of the tenements has given the children personal impulses akin to animal instincts. They learn to defend themselves from violence, and a primitive survival instinct directs their behaviour.

When *Maggie* appeared in 1893, literary realism had become the dominant mode of discourse among the most respected American novelists. Many who advocated realism nevertheless believed that literature should function to refine, improve, educate, and acculturate mankind. A depiction of men and women living out their baser instincts seemed to serve no elevating purpose, and many were at a loss to understand *Maggie* or appreciate what Crane was doing. Crane's reviewers saw he was doing something which went beyond realism but were not sure how to label his discursive approach. One called it 'aggressive realism' and another 'stern realism'. A. G. Sedgwick labelled Crane a writer of the 'animalistic school', defining animalism as 'a species of realism which deals with man considered as an animal, capable of hunger, thirst, lust, cruelty, vanity, fear, sloth, predacity, greed, and other passions and appetites that make him kin to the brutes, but which neglects, so far as possible, any higher qualities which distinguish him from his four-footed relatives, such as humor, thought, reason, aspiration, affection, morality, and religion' (*M* 21–2).

While Sedgwick's term animalism never really stuck, his definition of it is not inapplicable to literary naturalism, yet that term, too, inadequately describes Crane's work. Émile Zola – the foremost exemplar of literary naturalism – combined determinism with a preponderance of detail to overwhelm his readers. Much the same could be said about the prominent American naturalist writers Frank Norris and Theodore Dreiser. The most exemplary naturalistic novels require readers to see how every event and encounter contributes to the protagonist's inevitable fate and the story's inevitable outcome. While *Maggie* does contain some heavy-handed, naturalistic passages (Arnold Bennett observed, 'To read *Maggie* is to put one's ears into the bell of a cornet blown by giant lungs'), Crane's technique differs considerably (*M* 22). He is much more selective about the detail he includes.

Hamlin Garland, to name another American naturalist author, coined the term 'veritism', which, as Garland defined it, accurately describes Crane's technique, yet, like Sedgwick's animalism, the term never really entered the critical vocabulary. According to Garland, veritism combines local colour with literary impressionism. *Maggie* might be aligned with the local colour movement, for Crane captures the ambience and argot of one particular locale, New York's Lower East Side. The local colour movement, however, was generally associated with outlying, rural areas, not the city. The Sullivan County sketches can be identified with the local colour movement; *Maggie* cannot. The other component to Garland's veritism, impressionism, may be the best way to characterize Crane's style. As Joseph Conrad describes Crane's technique, 'His eye is very individual and his expression satisfies me artistically. He is certainly *the* impressionist and his temperament is curiously unique'.[1] A key difference between realism and literary impressionism is that realists seek to render their subject objectively while impressionistic writers create a subjective picture, depicting a scene the way they see it. Crane's descriptions are realistic, yet they are also highly personal and very selective. He picks and chooses his details, excising the unnecessary and compressing much information into a brief amount of space.

After the early chapters describing Maggie as a child, Crane skips several intervening years and, in chapter 5, depicts her grown up. In the tenements, one scarcely expects anything save ugliness and depravity, so it is something of a surprise to discover that Maggie grows into a beautiful young woman. Chapter 5 begins: 'The girl, Maggie, blossomed in a mud puddle. She grew to be a most rare and wonderful production of a tenement district, a pretty girl' (*M* 49). Like many young, unmarried women of the time, Maggie takes a job at a local factory, where she sits at a sewing machine all day making shirt collars and cuffs. Her life settles into routine, which is broken when Jimmie brings his friend Pete home one day. Though not exactly handsome, Pete has a personal bearing and a sense of bravado Maggie finds alluring. Desperate to escape the tenements, she lets her imagination envision a way out and sees Pete as 'the beau ideal of a man'. Her 'dim thoughts' search 'for far away lands where, as God says, the little hills sing together in the morning. Under the trees of her dream-gardens there had always walked a lover' (*M* 52). As in much of Crane's early writings, the personal imagination helps interpret experience yet, in so doing, idealizes it. Furthermore, Crane's diction suggests that Maggie's imagination has been shaped by her reading. Her thoughts echo the language of the Book of Psalms.

Contemporary popular culture further influences Maggie's imagination and thus shapes her view of the world. Pete takes her to a beer garden, where Maggie is awestruck by the gaudiness and glitter of the place. She has never seen anything like it, and the experience confirms her hope that Pete is the one who will take her from the tenements to a better world. As their courtship progresses, he often takes Maggie to the theatre, and the sentimental melodramas that prevail give her stereotypical images of men and women, which she naively interprets as possible versions of reality. She frequently leaves the theatre 'with raised spirits': 'She rejoiced at the way in which the poor and virtuous eventually surmounted the wealthy and wicked. The theater made her think. She wondered if the culture and refinement she had seen imitated, perhaps grotesquely, by the heroine on the stage, could be acquired by a girl who lived in a tenement house and worked in a shirt factory' (*M* 62).

Every time she returns home, however, she must face her raving, drunken mother, who abuses Maggie for going out with Pete. According to the day's social conventions, Maggie has little choice save to remain with her mother. At the time, young women, whether or not they worked, continued living with their parents until they married, when they stopped working to make a home of their own. Those few women who chose to live by themselves or shared flats with others were known as 'women adrift' and were frequently viewed as promiscuous and unsavoury. The reality of life in the tenements with her mother is more than Maggie can stand, especially compared with the ideal life she imagines with Pete. Consequently, she does what good girls were not supposed to do: she acquiesces to her lover's demands. Crane does not convey Maggie's actions in so many words, yet he does make the situation clear. Fiercely haranguing her daughter one evening, Maggie's mother yells, 'Go teh hell an' good riddance' (*M* 65). With extraordinary verbal economy, Crane follows Mary Johnson's harangue with a two-word paragraph, which closes the chapter: 'She went'.

Maggie sees nothing particularly wrong with having left her family for Pete: 'She did not feel like a bad woman. To her knowledge she had never seen any better' (*M* 74). While she may not have felt so, others begin to perceive her differently. Seeing her frequently at the beer garden with Pete, other men recognize her for what she is, and she becomes the object of their gaze: 'Grey-headed men, wonderfully pathetic in their dissipation, stared at her through clouds. Smooth cheeked boys, some of them with faces of stone and mouths of sin, not merely so pathetic as the grey heads, tried to find the girl's eyes in the smoke wreaths' (*M* 74). Maggie can feel the leers of other men and knows what they mean, yet she still sees herself as being above other women in her situation, for she continues to imagine a future with Pete.

Her world is destroyed, however, when Nellie enters the picture. An old girlfriend of Pete's, Nellie is a woman of experience. She is 'painted with no apparent paint' and can look 'clear-eyed through the stares of the men' (*M* 78). Out with Maggie one night, Pete meets Nellie and leaves with her. Maggie finds herself a victim. She was seduced, and now she has been abandoned. Seduced and abandoned: these words could be found in a contemporary survey of prostitutes in answer to a question asking why they had turned to prostitution. They were also used to explain why young, unmarried women committed suicide. With nowhere else to go, Maggie tries to return home, but her mother throws her out.

Several months intervene between chapter 16, in which Mary Johnson rejects her daughter, and chapter 17, which depicts Maggie's last night. Unquestionably the finest chapter in the book, chapter 17 may also constitute the finest description of a prostitute in American literature. Other writers before Crane had described female characters who had been seduced and abandoned and who had traced their descent into prostitution at great length. Crane had the insight to exclude the intervening detail, omitting precisely how Maggie had descended into prostitution. Instead, he skips several months in her story and only depicts her after that much time had passed and she has become an experienced prostitute.

After establishing the setting at the chapter's start – a rainy night, the theatres letting out – Crane describes Maggie's appearance on the street, using a generic description instead of her name: 'A girl of the painted cohorts of the city went along the street. She threw changing glances at men who passed her, giving smiling invitations to men of rural or untaught pattern and usually seeming sedately unconscious of the men with a metropolitan seal upon their faces' (*M* 87). Now experienced, Maggie no longer shirks the male gaze; she invites it and even manipulates it. She also has a certain procedure she undergoes. She starts with the most crowded, brightly lit street where the most well-to-do men can be found. Only if unsuccessful there does she resort to the darker, less crowded streets. This night, she has no particular luck. She approaches one man after another, and each refuses her for one reason or another. Her route takes her to a block that ends at the East River. 'She went into the blackness of the final block. The shutters of the tall buildings were closed like grim lips. The structures seemed to have eyes that looked over her, beyond her, at other things' (*M* 89). Finally, a man advances toward her:

> When almost to the river the girl saw a great figure. On going forward she perceived it to be a huge fat man in torn and greasy garments. His grey hair straggled down over his forehead. His small, bleared eyes, sparkling from amidst great rolls of red fat, swept eagerly over the girl's upturned face. He laughed, his brown, disordered teeth gleaming under a grey, grizzled moustache from which beer-drops dripped. His whole body gently quivered and shook like that of a dead jelly fish. Chuckling and leering, he followed the girl of the crimson legions. (*M* 89)

Crane's editors at Appleton found this passage so offensive that they expurgated it when they republished *Maggie* in 1896. The sight of this greasy fat man is more than Maggie can stand. Rather than go with him, she chooses to kill herself and, to that end, jumps in the East River. Here, too, Crane's verbal economy is extraordinary. Instead of articulating Maggie's actions, he describes the physical results of it: 'At their feet the river appeared a deathly black hue. Some hidden factory sent up a yellow glare, that lit for a moment the waters lapping oilily against timbers. The varied sounds of life, made joyous by distance and seeming unapproachableness, came faintly and died away to a silence' (*M* 89).

In *George's Mother*, his second novel of life in the tenements of New York's Lower East Side, Crane brought Maggie Johnson back. He had obviously formed an attachment to his fictional creation and was reluctant to see her go. He may have revived her because he was interested in tying his work together in a similar way to that of Zola in his multi-volume Rougon-Macquart series, which traces the fortunes and misfortunes of one family's descendants. While the reference to Maggie Johnson in *George's Mother* may reflect Zola's influence on Crane, it also shows how Crane departs from his literary forebear. Zola links his works together on the basis of heredity. Only after establishing the heritage of his characters does he show how their environment influences their behaviour. Crane, on the other hand, links his two books together solely on the basis of environment. George Kelcey and Maggie Johnson live in the same tenement. For Crane, the notion of heredity disappears from the equation. Place links the two works together.

Meeting Maggie on the stairs of their tenement, George develops a crush and imagines taking Maggie away from her family and the tenements: 'He was relatively happy sometimes when Maggie's mother would get drunk and make terrific uproars. He used then to sit in the dark and make scenes in which he rescued the girl from her hideous environment' (*W* i. 138). Crane's use of the word environment here recalls the message he inscribed in presentation copies of *Maggie*. *George's Mother* reinforces ideas Crane had introduced in *Maggie*. George, too, interprets his world from a personal and solipsistic perspective. Mary Johnson's brutal behaviour toward her family makes him happy: in George's mind it enhances the likelihood that he will be able to rescue Maggie. He, too, is influenced by the popular culture, and he sees himself as a kind of dime novel hero who rescues a beautiful maiden from the clutches of evil. *George's Mother*, generally considered inferior to *Maggie*, is not without its adherents. Eric Solomon, whose discussion of the novel in *Stephen Crane, from Parody to Realism* may constitute the finest critical appreciation of *George's Mother*, calls it 'Crane's most penetrating psychological novel' and compares it with the work of Nathanael West.[2]

Both George Kelcey and Maggie Johnson are trapped by their environment, and both seek escape in the imagination. Both are strongly influenced by the popular culture, which provides them with unrealistic ideas and images of what life could be like outside the tenement district. Maggie's fascination with sentimental melodrama and George's interest in heroic dime novels allow them to see life as something that it is not. While providing a temporary escape from the squalor of their everyday lives, the popular culture prevents them from imagining more realistic ways to escape the tenements and thus helps to assure that they will be unable to escape the grim environment of the tenements, at least in this lifetime.

3

Black Riders

The title of Stephen Crane's first collection of verse, *The Black Riders and Other Lines*, functions similarly to much of his early belletristic writings, for it recalls the literature of an earlier time only to call that literature into question. Historically, the term 'Black Riders' referred to the Prussian patriots led by Adolf Lützow during the Wars of Liberation (1813), who swore to wear black until their country was free. The exploits of the Black Riders were best known from a poem by Karl Theodor Körner, 'Lutzow's Wild Chase', which circulated widely in Europe and America. After Lützow, the phrase 'black riders' came to refer to any heroic band of patriots who terrorized their enemies. In *The Scout: or, The Black Riders of Congaree*, for example, William Gilmore Simms told a story of black riders on the South Carolina frontier during the American Revolution. Simms's historical novel, first published in 1841, remained in print in cheap editions through Crane's adolescence, when the dime novelists took up the phrase. Consider Mark Wilton's *Iron-Armed Abe, the Hunchback Destroyer: or, The Black Riders' Terror* (1883) or Eugene T. Sawyer's *The Black Riders of Santos: or, The Terror of Wood River* (1889).

The Black Riders and Other Lines gathers sixty-eight brief, untitled poems, which are printed in all capitals. The opening poem lends its imagery to the title of the collection:

BLACK RIDERS CAME FROM THE SEA.
THERE WAS CLANG AND CLANG OF SPEAR AND SHIELD,
AND CLASH AND CLASH OF HOOF AND HEEL,
WILD SHOUTS AND THE WAVE OF HAIR
IN THE RUSH UPON THE WIND:
THUS THE RIDE OF SIN.

Crane's black riders, though still terrifying warriors, are almost complete abstractions. No longer flesh-and-blood defenders of a cause, they have become foreboding symbols more reminiscent of the Four Horsemen of the Apocalypse than Lützow's patriots. Originating in the sea and spurred on by the wind, Crane's black riders, sin personified, form an essential part of the natural world.

Borrowing the phrase from the pages of historical romance and using it for both the volume title and the central image of its opening poem, Crane took the black riders from an identifiable place and time and situated them in the indefinite realm of his poems, which occur any time between now and eternity and anywhere between here and the horizon. Minimizing his topical references, Crane removed man from his contemporary moorings and cast him into an abstract version of nature. Crane projected an everyman figure into much of his verse as a means of testing his reaction to the natural elements, which stubbornly remain indifferent toward him. The 'out of space, out of time' quality of Crane's verse recalls the poetry of Edgar Allan Poe; its spare quality anticipates the *vers libre* of Amy Lowell and the imagists.

In terms of form, *Black Riders* reminded contemporary readers of two of the most prominent poets in the history of American literature. With their absence of rhyme, irregular meter, and uneven line lengths, Crane's poems recall those of Walt Whitman. Reviewing *Black Riders*, Harry Thurston Peck called Crane 'the Aubrey Beardsley of poetry' and fancifully imagined 'if Walt Whitman had been caught young and subjected to aesthetic influences, it is likely that he would have mellowed his barbaric yawp to some such note as that which sounds in the poems that are now before us' (*CH* 63). As succinct word paintings, Crane's poems are also reminiscent of Emily Dickinson's. T. W. Higginson, Dickinson's posthumous editor, compared Crane's verse both to hers and Whitman's. 'As formless, in the ordinary sense, as the productions of Walt Whitman', Crane's poetry is 'in other respects the antipodes of his; while Whitman dilutes mercilessly, he condenses almost as formidably'. Crane, Higginson continued, 'grasps his thought as nakedly and simply as Emily Dickinson' (*CH* 68).

The unique typographical format Crane's publishers, Copeland and Day, chose for the volume enhances the modernity of his verse. Individually quite short, the poems, in Amy Lowell's words, 'spurted from the tip-top of the pages' (*Work* vi. x) and, therefore, left considerable white space toward the bottom of each. The publishers strongly believed that the meaning of a text should help to determine its physical appearance on the printed page. The capitalized lines, as Christopher Benfey observes in *The Double Life of Stephen Crane,* suggest the scare headlines of contemporary newspapers as well as another modern form of communication, the telegram.[1] Discussing the influence of Crane's verse on futurist poetry of the late 1920s and early 1930s, Jerome McGann has suggested that Crane's black riders can be seen as references to the printed characters themselves. McGann found the importance of the printed page significant enough to make Crane's title his own. In *Black Riders: The Visible Language of Modernism,* he argues that the white spaces in Crane's volume hold significance, too. Crane's poems take the form of vignettes that occur in otherwise desolate space, and the white spaces on the page reiterate the psychic vacancy of the verse.

Crane's philosophical outlook also anticipates modernist poetry. One contemporary reader, who was reminded of Thomas Hardy's *Jude the Obscure* as he read *Black Riders,* suggested that Crane's poetry epitomizes 'the bitterness of Mr. Hardy's pessimism, his keen, remorseless sense of the ironies of life, the passionate insurgence of his heart against Nature's injustice, and the revolt of his soul against this sad, mad world'.[2] Another called *Black Riders* 'an experiment suggesting Walt Whitman on the one hand and Friedrich Nietzsche on the other' (*CH* 74). The freedom Crane exhibits with poetic form, the unusual appearance of the printed poems, and the bleak, seemingly nihilistic vision, place his verse at the start of the literary modernism.

The following poem, the third in the collection, as another reader observed, 'might serve either as a *credo* for the modern pessimist or as a felicitous epigram at his expense' (*CH* 73):

IN THE DESERT
I SAW A CREATURE, NAKED, BESTIAL,
WHO, SQUATTING UPON THE GROUND,

HELD HIS HEART IN HIS HANDS,
AND ATE OF IT.
I SAID, 'IS IT GOOD, FRIEND?'
'IT IS BITTER – BITTER', HE ANSWERED;
'BUT I LIKE IT
'BECAUSE IT IS BITTER,
'AND BECAUSE IT IS MY HEART'.

'In the Desert' transmogrifies the ordinary into the extraordinary. It adapts a commonplace figurative phrase – 'Eat your heart out' – and literalizes it to stress its grotesque quality. Generally spoken by one who has to one who has not, the traditional saying conveys intense feelings of envy. While antagonistic, it nevertheless assumes a relationship between two people. Unmotivated by envy or, for that matter, any other external stimulus, Crane's beast-like man eats his own heart for no apparent reason. He relishes the act of self-consumption in which he is engaged. His behaviour suggests that life is so bereft of meaning that modern man must paradoxically resort to self-destruction in order to satisfy the self.

Like 'In the Desert', many of the poems that comprise *Black Riders* are constructed as dramatized encounters between the speaker of the poem and a solitary person he meets by chance. 'In a Lonely Place' parallels 'In the Desert' in terms of its structure yet, unlike 'In the Desert', it does posit the existence of others because it makes reference to a specific medium of mass communication:

IN A LONELY PLACE,
I ENCOUNTERED A SAGE
WHO SAT, ALL STILL,
REGARDING A NEWSPAPER.
HE ACCOSTED ME:
'SIR, WHAT IS THIS?'
THEN I SAW THAT I WAS GREATER,
AYE, GREATER THAN THIS SAGE.
I ANSWERED HIM AT ONCE,
'OLD, OLD MAN, IT IS THE WISDOM OF THE AGE'.
THE SAGE LOOKED UPON ME WITH ADMIRATION.

The opening prepositional phrase imparts a feeling of isolation, yet the old man's behaviour – looking at a newspaper – reiterates an activity hundreds of thousands of people in

Crane's New York engaged in every day. The lonely place the poet mentions is not the middle of a desert but the heart of the city. People who open newspapers as soon as they take their seats on streetcars or park benches construct lonely places of their own, using the newspaper as a makeshift wall to isolate themselves from others. The poem's opening thus comments on the paradoxical nature of existence in the modern urban world. The crowded city is little more than a vast matrix of lonely places. 'In a Lonely Place' provides a good example of how the physical appearance of the printed page in *Black Riders* reinforces Crane's themes. Much as his poems appear as isolated texts amidst a vacancy of white, a newspaper held before the face in the modern urban world constitutes a printed text floating in anonymous space.

In Crane's day, as in our own, people generally accepted what they read in the papers without question and let the mass media shape what they thought. In a poem included in his second collection of verse, *War Is Kind*, Crane characterizes the newspaper as, among other things, 'a market / Where wisdom sells its freedom / And melons are crowned by the crowd' (*W* x. 52). Like those who read the *Boston Evening Transcript* in T. S. Eliot's poem of the same name, Crane's newspaper readers generally 'sway in the wind like a field of wheat'. The old sage of 'In a Lonely Place', on the other hand, questions the meaning of the medium. Having never seen a newspaper before, he cannot discern its significance simply by looking at it. Instead, he must ask for clarification. The speaker exhibits an ironic self-satisfaction in the superiority he presumes over the old sage. Identifying the newspaper as a vehicle of wisdom, the speaker, of course, identifies himself as a fool, and the sage, paradoxically, seems more sagacious for his ignorance.

Ironically identifying the newspaper as a source of wisdom, Crane implicitly questions all sources of wisdom and all those who claim to be wise. Reminiscent of Whitman's 'When I Heard the Learned Astronomer', a subsequent poem in *Black Riders* has its speaker encounter a learned man, with dubious consequences:

A LEARNED MAN CAME TO ME ONCE.
HE SAID, 'I KNOW THE WAY, – COME'.

AND I WAS OVERJOYED AT THIS.
TOGETHER WE HASTENED.
SOON, TOO SOON, WERE WE
WHERE MY EYES WERE USELESS,
AND I KNEW NOT THE WAYS OF MY FEET.
I CLUNG TO THE HAND OF MY FRIEND;
BUT AT LAST HE CRIED, 'I AM LOST'.

Whitman had set 'When I Heard the Learned Astronomer' in a place where many middle-class Americans in the nineteenth century went for both entertainment and edification, the public lecture hall. Unlike other members of his astronomer's generally appreciative audience, the speaker of Whitman's poem tires of listening to him discuss the heavens in abstract mathematical terms, leaves the lecture hall, and ventures outdoors to witness the heavens for himself. Outside within 'the mystical moist night-air', Whitman's speaker makes himself comfortable and, from time to time, gazes 'in perfect silence at the stars'.

The edifying lecture gave contemporary audiences an opportunity for both entertainment and what would later be called continuing education. Critiquing the learned astronomer, Whitman does not critique the value of self-motivated education. Rather, he questions the commodification of knowledge. In Whitman's view, astronomy, or any other field of knowledge for that matter, is not something that could or should be packaged as entertainment and marketed to mass audiences. Rather, self-education is an individual pursuit, and the only requisites are self-confidence and an observant eye. Whitman's criticism notwithstanding, the edifying lecture continued to be a popular form of bourgeois entertainment through the nineteenth century. Among Stephen Crane's early newspaper contributions are reports of summertime lectures delivered at Asbury Park, New Jersey, and another poem in *Black Riders* ironically begins, 'The sage lectured brilliantly'.

Unlike Whitman's, the speaker of 'A learned man came to me once' knows nothing of edifying lectures and has no confidence in his own capacity for enlightenment. Consequently, he eagerly welcomes the learned man who approaches him. He follows the man of learning into the darkness, happy to have him leading the way. Before long, however, the learned man loses himself in the darkness and must confess his ignorance, too. Though Whitman's poem questions the value of the public lecture, it nevertheless celebrates the possibility of personal enlightenment. Crane, on the other hand, takes his readers to a place with no exit. Learning can provide no guidance, and the individual is helpless to find his way through the metaphorical darkness he faces. The traditional virtues that had become associated with the American national character and had been exemplified in the literature from Captain John Smith through Ralph Waldo Emerson to Whitman – hard work, stick-to-it-tiveness, self-reliance – no longer apply. Neither learning nor traditional values can save modern man from the dark morass into which he is mired.

Though Crane set much of his poetry within highly abstract versions of nature, many of his poems develop themes he set forth in his naturalistic fiction. Some reiterate the heredity-versus-environment debate. 'Once I Saw Mountains Angry', for example, implicitly questions the capacity of heredity to withstand the force of environment:

ONCE I SAW MOUNTAINS ANGRY,
AND RANGED IN BATTLE-FRONT.
AGAINST THEM STOOD A LITTLE MAN;
AYE, HE WAS NO BIGGER THAN MY FINGER.
I LAUGHED, AND SPOKE TO ONE NEAR ME,
'WILL HE PREVAIL?'
'SURELY', REPLIED THIS OTHER;
'HIS GRANDFATHERS BEAT THEM MANY TIMES'.
THEN DID I SEE MUCH VIRTUE IN GRANDFATHERS, – AT LEAST, FOR THE LITTLE MAN
WHO STOOD AGAINST THE MOUNTAINS.

The situation of a little man confronting mountains recalls Crane's earlier sketch, 'The Mesmeric Mountain'. While the description of the mountain-confronting person as a 'little man' suggests his physical stature in the sketch, in 'Once I Saw Mountains Angry', the description reflects man's relative insignificance in comparison to nature. It also reflects the speaker's visual perspective. The man looks little because he stands far from the speaker. The mountain range, which stands even further in the distance, resembles a battalion of soldiers.

Giving the speaker someone to talk to, Crane creates an audience for the little man, whose activity thus takes on the quality of a spectacle.

It seems impossible for the little man to battle the mountains successfully, so impossible that the situation is laughable. When the speaker learns that the little man's grandfathers had successfully battled the mountains, however, he acknowledges the possibility of his success. 'Once I Saw Mountains Angry' denies the little man any hope of conquest until the success of his grandfathers becomes known. Giving the grandfathers credit, Crane denies the power of the individual to overcome the obstacles he faces. Human behaviour seems little more than a chemical process, the working out of what is in the blood.

One of Crane's most memorable verses encapsulates a similar situation:

I SAW A MAN PURSUING THE HORIZON;
ROUND AND ROUND THEY SPED.
I WAS DISTURBED AT THIS;
I ACCOSTED THE MAN.
'IT IS FUTILE', I SAID,
'YOU CAN NEVER –'
'YOU LIE', HE CRIED,
AND RAN ON.

The poem almost seems to be a redaction of 'Once I Saw Mountains Angry'. Crane flattened out the distant mountains, recognizing the horizon as ultimately much more intimidating. Regardless how tall or steep, mountains can ultimately be scaled, yet no one can catch the horizon.

Sherwood Anderson saw Crane doing something in *Black Riders* very different from his literary predecessors and compared the activities of the little men in his poems to the creative process. According to Anderson, Crane's poems are 'pure colour, experiments, a man finding his way, feeling his way' (*Work* xi. xiv). Anderson's words reinforce the modernity of Crane's verse. To be sure, 'I Saw a Man Pursuing the Horizon' articulates a very different attitude from what Henry David Thoreau had voiced a half-century before. In *A Week on the Concord and Merrimack Rivers,* Thoreau looked toward the west and 'resolved to scale the blue wall which bounded the western horizon'. Thoreau could imaginatively reach the horizon and even transcend man's physicality. Crane's running man, it seems, leads a life of frenzied desperation. He represents man's capacity for self-delusion as he continues his pursuit regardless of the futility of his task.

4

Image and Emblem in *The Red Badge of Courage*

Surveying the prehistory of cinema, Brian Winston found that a recent study of the subject fell short of ideal because it failed to answer a fundamental question: 'Why 1895?'.[1] To paraphrase and, in so doing, expand Winston's question: What factors – social, cultural, technological, discursive – came together in the mid 1890s to create the conditions necessary for cinema to happen at that particular moment? This question assumes that important cultural developments occur when they do because they represent a simultaneous coming together of a variety of disparate factors. This question could also be levelled at *The Red Badge of Courage*, the first edition of which appeared in 1895. Not only can the same question be asked of both cinema and *Red Badge*, the answer in each case may be much the same, for Crane's Civil War novel – the finest war novel in the language, some say – embodies a visual sensibility not dissimilar to that of the cinema.

While using the cinema as a model to understand *Red Badge* may seem anachronistic, it is important to realize that by the time Crane was writing, moving images as entertainment had already become a part of the popular culture. For decades, panoramas had been attracting mass audiences. Long rolls of fabric onto which were painted scenes illustrating a variety of historical or geographical subjects, panoramas were stretched across a stage and unfurled as audiences witnessed the scenes they depicted. Great battles of the Civil War remained the most popular subjects for panoramas from the end of the war to the end of the century. The most ambitious ones attempted to depict thousands of soldiers. Though familiar with the panorama as popular entertainment, Crane did not take it as a model for his war novel. Whereas Civil War panoramas strived for epic effects, the *Red Badge* is deliberately narrow in scope.

A reference to panoramas in 'Killing His Bear', another of Crane's Sullivan County sketches, prefigures *Red Badge* in terms of the way contemporary visual culture could be subsumed within a personal vision, however. Describing how the little man of the story foresaw the results of his hunting experience, Crane wrote: 'Swift pictures of himself in a thousand attitudes under a thousand combinations of circumstances, killing a thousand bears, passed panoramically through him' (*W* viii. 250). Crane's little man anticipates the behaviour of his little soldier in *Red Badge*. The swiftness with which the images move through his mind anticipates motion pictures.

Before Thomas Edison began marketing his kinetoscope, people had other technical ways to view moving images; the camera obscura, marketed as a device for popular amusement, could be found at various resort locations in the United States including Ocean Grove, New Jersey, a vacation spot Crane described in his 1892 sketch 'Joys of Seaside Life'. Discussing the various amusements available there, he paid particular attention to the camera obscura: 'People enter a small wooden building and stand in a darkened room, gazing at the surface of a small round table, on which appear reflections made through a lens in the top of the tower of all that is happening in the vicinity at the time. One gets a miniature of everything that occurs in the streets, on the boardwalk or on the hotel-porches. One can watch the bathers gambolling in the surf or peer at the deck of a passing ship' (*W* viii. 512–13).

'Joys of Seaside Life' records the fascination with moving images that existed before motion pictures began being exhibited. While early motion pictures often gave audiences views of various faraway places and events, the popularity of the camera obscura as a sideshow indicates that moving images were fascinating in and of themselves. The images people saw reflected from the surface of the circular table, after all, came from their present surroundings. They easily could have walked outside the wooden building and witnessed the source of the moving images much more clearly than the images themselves. Instead they were intrigued to see how their world could be mediated, represented, and projected. Crane's gambolling bathers suggest that the camera obscura also sanctioned an otherwise unacceptable voyeurism. While staring at bathers was improper, staring at moving images of bathers within the confines of the camera obscura building was acceptable and even expected.

The visual culture significantly influenced the critical discourse in Crane's day, and some of his reviewers used critical terminology linking his work to the moving image. Harold Frederic, for one, found that *Red Badge* had the 'effect of a photographic revelation' and compared Crane's verbal imagery to that of a camera that could record movement in 'the same way battle painters depict horses in motion, not as they actually move, but as it has been agreed by numberless generations of draughtsmen to say that they move. At last, along comes a Muybridge, with his instantaneous camera, and shows that the real motion is entirely different' (*CH* 119). Eadweard Muybridge ingeniously proved, through a series of stop-motion photographs, that a galloping horse did indeed lift all four legs from the ground simultaneously. Much as Muybridge was able to capture motion using still images, Crane could capture moving images via the static medium of the printed word. The language of other reviewers confirms the affinity between Crane's novel and motion pictures. Another characterized *Red Badge* as a 'precipitate outpouring of lively pictures'. Writing two years later, that is, after motion pictures began being exhibited, a British reviewer offered a general observation on Crane's visual imagery. 'Lifelike as Mr. Crane's pictures are', he observed, 'they have something of the spasmodic jerkiness of the kinetoscope' (*CH* 200, 205).

The opening sentence of the novel has the quality of the opening scene of a motion picture: 'The cold passed reluctantly from the earth and the retiring fogs revealed an army stretched out on the hills, resting'. In a fond appreciation of *Red Badge*, Nigel Andrews, film critic for the *Financial Times*, likens this sentence to 'the opening scene of a good movie, only better'.[2] Andrews follows a number of earlier commentators who found in *Red Badge* an affinity with motion pictures. After quoting the novel's opening in his monograph *Stephen Crane*, Edwin Cady, who elsewhere emphasizes the montage-like quality of Crane's prose, asserts that Crane 'handles point of view more like a movie camera than perhaps any predecessor had done'.[3] Throughout the novel Crane's choice of words frequently conveys two qualities characteristic of motion-picture spectatorship, the projection and the visual perception of the moving image.

Henry Fleming or 'the youth', as Crane terms his soldier-protagonist, has a vivid imagination. Hearing stories from other soldiers and reading accounts of the war prior to enlisting in the Union army, Henry easily pictures what war must be like: 'His busy mind had drawn for him large pictures, extravagant in colour, lurid with breathless deeds' (*RB* 3). Not only does he imagine the broad sweep of battle, he also foresees much detail in close-up. The graphic stories of those who have seen action allow him to envision 'red, live bones sticking out through slits in the faded uniforms' (*RB* 7). Furthermore, Crane's narrative point of view reinforces Henry's viewpoint. Though told from the third person, *Red Badge* is usually focalized from Henry's perspective. In other words, a third-person narrator articulates Henry's thoughts and verbalizes his mental imagery.

Though Henry sees the war in his mind's eye before going into battle, he perceives it as a spectator, not a participant. He foresees battle scenes, yet he cannot see himself in them. After enlisting, yet before entering battle, Henry, along with the rest of his unit, must wait almost interminably before entering battle. During that time he tries hard to imagine how he will react yet still cannot do so. His inability to envision himself in battle makes him uneasy, so he resolves to observe everything closely in order to gather the information that will allow him to foresee his behaviour in battle. Generally speaking, Henry's process of information-gathering is non-verbal. His eyes function as his primary sense organs. He often fixes his gaze on the characteristic icons of battle and thus privileges the familiar and the recognizable. Upon seeing batteries being lead by their standard bearers in the distance, for example, Henry devotes his attention to their flags and, in so doing, feels 'the old thrill at the sight of the emblems' (*RB* 29). His attention to the flag in this case establishes a precedent for his subsequent behaviour. The emblems of battle become the visual signs by which he navigates himself through the ensuing conflict.

After surviving his first skirmish, Henry experiences tremendous relief. As a result, he no longer feels the need to envision how he will react in battle because he now concludes that he does indeed have the courage to face conflict. Self-satisfied, he can perceive himself from an external point of view and picture himself as a combat soldier: 'Standing as if apart from himself, he viewed that last scene. He perceived that the man who had fought thus was magnificent' (*RB* 30). His brief personal experience allows him to do something that his third-hand information gathering had not, to envision war as a participant and not merely as a spectator.

The pictures Henry can now see in his mind's eye are more recollections of recent events than projections of the future, however. They do not prepare him for further combat. Having mistaken the initial skirmish for the entire battle, he is unprepared for the following action. After assuming he has survived the battle without losing his nerve, he must now confront additional dangers. Neither his experience nor his imagination has prepared him for the new challenge. He loses courage and flees. After reaching a safe distance, however, he turns to witness the action he has fled: 'Then he began to run in the direction of the battle. He saw that it was an ironical thing for him to be running thus toward that which he had been at such pains to avoid. But he said, in substance, to himself that if the earth and the moon were about to clash, many persons would doubtless plan to get upon roofs to witness the collision' (*RB* 38). Those who have studied the prehistory of the cinema have identified the *badaud* or gawker as the nineteenth-century precursor of the cinema spectator, and this is the role Henry assumes upon fleeing the battle, as Crane's diction makes clear: 'He stood, regardant, for a moment. His eyes had an awe-struck expression. He gawked in the direction of the fight' (*RB* 39).

Henry continues to gawk as he wanders aimlessly behind the lines. His gawking does have a vague purpose, however: he seeks a way to reintegrate himself within the battle. Witnessing a line of wounded soldiers, Henry perceives them with a pang of envy: 'He conceived persons with torn bodies to be peculiarly happy. He wished that he, too, had a wound, a little red badge of courage' (*RB* 42). Callously, Henry perceives battle wounds not in terms of pain inflicted but in terms of symbolic value. Not even the sight of his mortally wounded friend Jim Conklin, whose side 'looked as if it had been chewed by wolves' (*RB* 45), dissuades Henry from his fascination with the emblematic value of battle scars.

The visible wound, an emblem of war rather than war itself, provides the key for Henry to imagine himself in battle. Understanding the results of battle abstractly, he can envision himself within the conflict:

> Swift pictures of himself, apart, yet in himself, came to him – a blue desperate figure leading lurid charges with one knee forward and a broken blade high – a blue, determined figure standing before a crimson and steel assault, getting calmly killed on a high place before the eyes of all. He thought of the magnificent pathos of his dead body. . . . He thought that he was about to start fleetly for the front. Indeed, he saw a picture of himself, dust-stained, haggard, panting, flying to the front at the proper moment to seize and throttle the dark, leering witch of calamity. (*RB* 51)

Seeing himself as a brave soldier, Henry creates an ideal image analogous to the emblems that so capture his attention. Like the emblems of war, Henry's pictures of himself are idealized abstractions. These personal images as a brave soldier become so obvious to him that, much like the cinema, they appear as moving pictures projected before a vast audience: 'He saw himself chasing a thought-phantom across the sky before the assembled eyes of mankind' (*RB* 56).

Though recovering the ability to envision himself in battle, Henry is still not ready to return to combat. Encountering a group of soldiers scattering from the front lines, he seeks answers to explain the confusion. He becomes so desperate for information that he clutches one of the soldiers and refuses to let go. Struggling to free himself, the other soldier swings his rifle, which hits Henry in the head with sufficient force to break the skin and cause some bleeding. Reuniting with his regiment late that evening, Henry tells a different story to explain the cause of his wound: 'I got shot' (*RB* 62). With these three words, Henry creates a narrative fiction to explain the cause of his wound and, in so doing, transforms an injury borne of confusion and panic into a red, yet surreptitious badge of courage.

As members of his regiment accept Henry's fiction as truth, he becomes quite self-satisfied, and his imagination lets him project himself as a hero to an audience of eager onlookers. He imagines himself 'in a room of warm tints telling tales to listeners' and foresees 'his gaping audience picturing him as the central figure in blazing scenes' (*RB* 73). Henry has transformed himself from a gawker to the object of gawkers. His wound lends credence to his lie, and Henry, now reunited with his unit, has successfully obscured his cowardly desertion.

Henry's behaviour beyond this point in the novel has been open to much critical debate. The controversy that has dogged *The Red Badge of Courage* over the course of its history involves the issue of Henry Fleming's maturity. Does Henry mature over the course of the novel, turning himself from frightened youth into courageous soldier? Or does he remain immature and self-centred even as he seems to enter combat? While the version of *Red Badge* edited by Henry Binder from Crane's original manuscript in the 1970s would seem to have answered the question once and for all, the controversy rages nonetheless.

Instead of asking whether Henry matures in battle, perhaps it would be more productive to ask how he copes with the dangers of battle. No longer fleeing from combat in a physical sense, Henry copes with danger through flights of fancy: he faces combat by enacting personal fantasies of bravery. Having formed mental images of battle, he now projects himself into those images.

The emblems of battle provide the connection between the real war and the combat Henry imagined. The flag becomes something he can cling to for its emblematic value. As Kermit Vanderbilt and Daniel Weiss have observed, the flag is Henry's fantasized charm against danger, and he endows it with extraordinary power.[4] Articulating what the flag means to Henry, Crane observes, 'It was a creation of beauty and invulnerability. It was a goddess, radiant, that bended its form with an imperious gesture to him. It was a woman, red and white, hating and loving, that called him with the voice of his hopes. Because no harm could come to it, he endowed it with power. He kept near as if it could be a saver of lives and an imploring cry went from his mind' (*RB* 88).

The flag has such power that it can animate the dead. Seeing the colour sergeant perish, Henry and a fellow soldier grab the flagstaff simultaneously: 'He made a spring and a clutch at the pole. At the same instant, his friend grabbed it from the other side. They jerked at it, stout and furious, but the colour-serjeant was dead and the corpse would not relinquish its trust. For a moment, there was a grim encounter. The dead man, swinging with bended back seemed to be obstinately tugging, in ludicrous and awful ways for the possession of the flag' (*RB* 88). Their struggle more closely resembles a boys' game than it does proper behaviour in battle. Henry finally captures the flag for himself by pushing his friend away.

The flag, combined with his surreptitious wound, combine to make Henry seem a ferocious soldier. Both flag and wound, after all, serve the same function in his mind. Both are emblems of war. Even as his emblems allow him to re-enter battle, Henry remains a spectator, however. Crane wrote, 'The youth, still the bearer of the colours, did not feel his idleness. He was deeply absorbed as a spectator. The crash and swing of the great drama made him lean forward – intent eyed, his face working in small contortions. Sometimes, he prattled, words coming unconsciously from him in grotesque exclamations. He did not know that he breathed; that the flag hung silently over him, so absorbed was he' (*RB* 99). Henry gawks in much the same way he had after running from battle. The difference is that, equipped with his emblems – red badge and red, white, and blue – he can imaginatively and actually project himself into battle.

Henry's seeming deeds of bravery become, for him, mental pictures to be viewed again and again:

> But the youth, regarding his procession of memory, felt gleeful and unregretting, for, in it, his public deeds were paraded in great and shining prominence. Those performances which had been witnessed by his fellows marched now in wide purple and gold,

> hiding various deflections. They went gaily, with music. It was pleasure to watch these things. He spent delightful minutes viewing the gilded images of memory. (*RB* 106)

What remains in his memory are not images of dead and dying, but images of himself. Henry has become the star of his own movie.

5

Love, Art, Work: *The Third Violet*

There is freedom in obscurity. Authors whose works remain unknown are free to write whatever they wish to write. Once they publish their first commercially successful book, however, they win the opportunity to support themselves with their pen yet often lose a fair measure of their artistic freedom. Readers develop expectations for the authors they admire; after enjoying one particular book, they expect its author to keep writing similar kinds of books. With the popular success of *The Red Badge of Courage,* first as a syndicated newspaper serial and then in book form, Crane acquired an excellent reputation as an author of war stories, and his newfound readers, by and large, expected him to keep writing war stories. What Crane lost in artistic freedom, however, he made up for in opportunity. Having achieved literary recognition as the author of *Red Badge,* he received numerous offers to contribute to both newspaper syndicates and the more elite literary magazines. From mid 1895 through mid 1896, Crane published several short stories pertaining to the Civil War, six of which he collected under the title *The Little Regiment and Other Episodes of the American Civil War*.

According to a rumour circulating around the time *The Little Regiment* was published, Crane said he would write no more war stories. On 25 October 1896, the same day Jeannette Gilder reported this rumour in the New York *World,* Crane's fourth novel, *The Third Violet,* was starting to appear in syndication in newspapers across the United States. *The Third Violet* marks a significant departure for the author of *The Red Badge of Courage* and *The Little Regiment*, as contemporary reviewers were quick to notice. After its publication in book form the following year, one commented, 'Inverting the procedure of Virgil, who passed from bucolic strains to the *horrentia Martis arma*, Mr. Stephen Crane has in *The Third Violet* turned aside from the battlefield into the realm of the pastoral idyll' (*CH* 204).

The pastoral setting reflects both Crane's state of mind as he began *The Third Violet* and the environment in which he wrote it. He started writing the novel soon after Appleton had published *Red Badge* in late September 1895 to instant acclaim. Neither Crane's disappointing experience with the self-published *Maggie* two years before nor the recent publication of *The Black Riders* had prepared him for the praise he was receiving for his new book. He was uneasy with all the attention and did not remain in New York City. Instead he decided to retreat to Hartwood, his brother's hunting lodge in Sullivan County, a place that offered him much pleasure yet also provided an opportunity to write. Shortly after arriving, Crane expressed his pleasure in a letter to a friend: 'The brown October woods are simply great. . . . What can be finer than a fine frosty morning, a runaway horse, and only the still hills to watch' (*C* i. 127).

The rural surroundings significantly shaped the novel's plot. *The Third Violet* tells the story of Billie Hawker, a young painter trained in Paris and now living and working in New York City, who visits his family farm in Sullivan County. Whereas other city folk visit the region to enjoy the recreational opportunities it has to offer, Billie travels to Sullivan County for the purpose of work, not play. He seeks to restore contact with his birthplace; his journey home represents his desire to return to fundamentals in his art. He plans to spend the summer painting landscapes, which ideally will allow him to integrate his upbringing with his vocation. Arriving on the same train as Billie and planning to stay at the Hemlock Inn, a nearby resort hotel, a well-mannered young woman named Grace Fanhall has come fresh from New York society. Over the summer the two begin a courtship, which they attempt to renew after both return to the city. As their fondness for one another grows, Grace coyly presents Billie with a violet as an emblem of her affection. The gift, combined with the novel's title, establishes a modest amount of suspense, for it prompts the reader to wonder when and under what circumstances the second and third ones will appear. Perhaps a more important trio than the three violets, however, is the group of three linked themes that underlie the novel.

By the time he came to *The Third Violet*, Stephen Crane had reached approximately the same point in his literary career as his protagonist has reached in his career as an artist. With *Red Badge*, Crane was establishing his reputation as an important author, but to that end he had had to compromise the novel's original text significantly to make it more appealing to his readers. Helen Sargent Hitchcock, the wife of Crane's editor at Appleton, inscribed her copy of *Red Badge* with the comment: 'Two versions of this book written, Mr Hitchcock made Crane rewrite it and this was the first published version' (*C* i. 173). Billie Hawker, fresh from art school, had entered the New York art scene only to find disappointment. It was not until he, too, had compromised himself and had begun doing commercial artwork that he began to establish a reputation for his artistic skill. As he tells Grace shortly after they become acquainted: 'Whenever you come upon tomatoes remember that they might once have been encompassed in my design. When first I came back from Paris I began to paint, but nobody wanted me to paint. My tomato-can designs met, however, with instant favor. Later, I got into green corn and asparagus' (*W* iii. 24, 421).

The Third Violet met with mixed reviews. John Berryman may have overstated the case when he characterized the British reception of *The Third Violet* in his biography of Crane as 'doggedly rapturous',[1] but generally speaking, British reviewers received the book more favourably than did their American counterparts. The *Critic*, an American weekly, called the novel a 'vacuous trifle' while the *Academy*, the well-respected British weekly, found that *The Third Violet* confirmed Crane's genius and concluded that 'for psychological insight, for dramatic intensity, and for potency of phrase he is already in the front rank of English and American writers of fiction' (*CH* 206, 201). The *Manchester Guardian* (18 May 1897), too, enjoyed the novel and appreciated how Crane appealed 'to the intelligence of his readers, whom he credits with enough imagination to fill in the purposed gaps in the story of the artist Hawker and the beautiful Miss Fanhall'. These comments reveal a shrewd understanding of Crane's deliberately elliptical style.

Since the early British reception, few have appreciated the novel. Some years ago, however, William Andrews suggested that one way to understand *The Third Violet* is to recognize what it says about the relationship between art and success.[2] Making his protagonist an artist yet naming him Hawker, Crane links art and commerce and, in so doing, signals the problematic nature of the artist in the modern world. It is insufficient for him to create art. He must also hawk his wares in the marketplace. Adding Grace Fanhall to the mix, Crane provides a third element and, in so doing, transforms *The Third Violet* into an inquiry about the relationships between love, art, and work.

The action begins as Billie and Grace arrive at the local railway station. As she asks him where the Hemlock Inn is, he becomes astonished with her appearance. He says to himself, 'Wouldn't I like to paint her, though. What a glance – oh, murder. The – the – the distance in her eyes' (*W* iii. 4). The encounter offers a glimpse into Billie's personality. Though he had travelled to Paris to study art, his experience there had apparently not made him a man of the world. He remains naive and has little idea how to react to or behave toward this attractive, refined young woman. Ignorant in matters of the heart, he uses what he knows – his work – to interpret his feelings toward Grace.

The morning after their arrival Billie, determined to start working, trudges outdoors with easel and palette to an overlook, where he begins the first of many landscapes he intends to paint this summer. Soon his old friend George Hollanden, also spending the summer at the Hemlock Inn, approaches. Decked out in white flannels, Hollanden walks into his friend's visual field, whereupon Billie exclaims, 'Hi, Hollie, get out of the colour-scheme' (*W* iii. 9). In terms of personality, Hollanden, a ne'r-do-well dandy, seems more appropriate for a Scott Fitzgerald novel than a Stephen Crane one. He, too, is an artist figure, of sorts, for he plys his trade as a contributor to the day's popular magazines. Hollanden represents a philosophy of work and art Billie continues to resist; that is, the artist who has abandoned all hope of creating art for art's sake and recognizes that his task is to create works to please the masses. Hollanden cynically sees himself as an author who writes magazine pieces that will be quickly published, sold, and read and just as quickly forgotten. He has long forsaken the high-minded values he formerly held. As he tells Billie, 'I started my career – my career, you understand – with a determination to be a prophet' and 'have ended in being an acrobat, a trained bear of the magazines, and a juggler of comic paragraphs' (*W* iii. 16). Hollanden functions as a foil for Billie. Though his experience as a commercial artist has jaded Billie, it has not made him cynical like his friend. Billie retains much hope for his art, and this summer excursion to his family farm represents Billie's attempt to recapture his artistic sensibilities.

Despite or, perhaps, because of Billie's ineptness in the ways of love and courtship, Grace becomes fond of him. His burgeoning love for her, combined with Hollie's continual interruptions, thwart his efforts to get any work done, however. Compounding his inability to concentrate on his work, Jem Oglethorpe, another beau of Grace's, visits Sullivan County to see her. The idea that Grace could fancy someone like Oglethorpe Billie finds outrageous. A successful businessman, Oglethorpe – no one would imagine calling him Oggie Oglethorpe – is a complete dullard in terms of understanding art. Regardless of the artist's chosen medium – words on a page or landscapes on canvas – what matters to Oglethorpe is the popularity of a work of art. For him, artistic value can be quantifiable: it is directly related to the number of people who appreciate it.

While it seems fairly obvious to others that Grace prefers Billie, he does not recognize how she feels. Even after she presents him with a second violet during Oglethorpe's stay in Sullivan County, Billie remains uncertain of her feelings and imagines her casting him aside for the likes of Oglethorpe. Grace's sudden departure from the Hemlock Inn reinforces Billie's fears. Soon after giving him the second violet, she returns home to New York City.

Billie's jealousy of Oglethorpe, uncertainty about Grace, and inability to articulate his feelings for her find release in his art.

Psychoanalytic thought can offer help toward understanding Billie. In his concluding comments to 'The Paths to Symptom-Formation', one of the *Introductory Lectures on Psychoanalysis*, Freud comments that the artist, generally speaking, is an introvert not far from neurosis. Oppressed by powerful instinctual needs, he desires to win honour, power, wealth, fame, and the love of women yet lacks the means for satisfying these desires. For those lacking artistic ability, the frustration resulting from unfulfilled desire can lead to neurotic behaviour, but the artist transfers his feelings of frustration to his art. The painting Billie creates after Grace leaves Sullivan County clearly embodies his desire for her, as his palette clearly reveals. The colour violet, by itself or separated into the primary colours of which it consists, dominates his palette. Choosing an hour when the atmosphere is 'a dark blue, like powder smoke in the shade of trees' and the western sky burns 'in strips of red', he paints 'with a wild face like a man who is killing' (*W* iii. 60). Unfulfilled love, Crane suggested, may find its outlet in violence or, in Billie's case, violence sublimated into work.

Hollanden, seeing his friend using purple to paint a shadow, asks Billie if the shadow he sees really looks purple to him. 'Certainly it does', Billie responds, 'or I wouldn't paint it so' (*W* iii. 61). Violet, besides symbolizing Grace's affection for Billie, colours not only his palette but also his perception. It influences both how he paints and how he sees what he paints. Reintroducing Hollanden at this moment in the story, Crane allows Billie to see how an audience might perceive a work of art inspired by his feelings of frustration toward Grace. The artist, according to Freud, understands how to recast his daydreams in order to make them lose what is too personal and repellent and to make it possible for others to enjoy what the artist creates. The true artist understands how to integrate deep feelings so that the work of art does not easily betray its sometimes highly personal sources of inspiration. Hollanden's reaction suggests that Billie has successfully sublimated his feelings toward Grace, for Hollanden does not interpret Billie's painting as an external manifestation of his emotional turmoil. Rather, he concludes that the painting reflects how Billie's visual perception differs from his own. Through his work,

Billie has successfully transmogrified his feelings of love and frustration into art.

The love Billie has felt for Grace during her presence in Sullivan County is exacerbated by the jealousy and melancholy he feels upon her absence. Consequently, he decides to return to the city. Learning of his decision, yet not knowing the reasons behind it, his parents discuss why he may be leaving. His mother says, 'I bet he's going back so's he can see that girl', whereupon his father responds, 'He says it's his work' (*W* iii. 61). At one level this humdrum exchange represents a typical conversation by a stereotypical Darby and Joan, yet in these few words Crane compounds much meaning. Fundamentally their words contrast male and female ways of knowing. Mrs Hawker interprets her son's departure intuitively and believes so strongly in her intuition that she expresses a desire to place a wager on it. Her husband, alternatively, relies on an external source of information and cites his son's words to indicate the motive behind his behaviour. The attitudes they convey make Mr and Mrs Hawker analogous to Billie and Grace. Like Mrs Hawker, Grace interprets Billie intuitively. Like his father, Billie needs external signs to interpret another's behaviour. Grace gives him violets, yet even these obvious emblems are inadequate. As his father relies on his son's words, Billie, too, needs verbal indicators to interpret another's behaviour. These Grace continually refuses to provide.

In New York City, Billie lives and works among a group of poor, young artists. His studio is adjacent to the seedy apartment where they live en masse. Billie's artist friends represent a different phase in the development of the artist, the idealistic period. They refuse to bow to commercial pressures and compromise their art for the sake of profit. Crane's depiction of these starving artists is not without ambiguity. They feign superiority over those who profit from their craft – 'more successful painters whose work they usually pronounced "Rotten" ' (*W* iii. 69) – but perhaps they simply lack the talent to be any more successful than they are. Billie, on the other hand, is an exception, for his artist friends generally admire his work and applaud his success, modest though it may be. Understanding their friend's attention to his work, they are surprised to discover how he has changed upon returning from Sullivan County. One, who sees Billie empty the two violets from an envelope and stare at them at length, recognizes a possible source of Billie's personal change. As Billie's early attempts to see Grace upon returning to the city fail, he becomes more despondent, and his artist-friends make conjectures regarding his behaviour. Some suggest his apparent depression and anger stem from a discussion about art 'with some pot-boiler . . . as if this was the final condition of human misery'. A more intuitive member of the gang refutes this idea and instead asserts, 'It's something connected with the now celebrated violets' (*W* iii. 80).

Billie and Grace eventually get together in the closing chapter of the novel, during which she presents him with the third violet. Overall, their meeting does not go smoothly, and he gallantly suggests that they should break off their relationship. Crane's closing sentence conveys her attitude toward his suggestion: 'Later, she told him that he was perfectly ridiculous' (*W* iii. 110).

Crane's conclusion is worthy of Henry James. Though the two had yet to meet, Crane demonstrates an affinity with his fellow novelist with this delightfully ambiguous concluding sentence. The sentence indicates that despite Billie's suggestion that they break off their relationship, they do see each other again, at which time Grace calls him ridiculous. Would this comment have been in jest or in earnest? Crane's tone seems playful yet the passage remains ambiguous. Did they continue their relationship? Freud would have said yes. The artist, having successfully created a work of art, makes it possible for others 'to derive consolation and alleviation from their own sources of pleasure in their unconscious which have become inaccessible to them; he earns their gratitude and admiration and he thus achieves *through* his phantasy what originally he had achieved only *in* his phantasy – honour, power and the love of women'. Billie has sublimated the frustrated love he has felt toward Grace in his work, which results in the production of art and facilitates their romance.

Understood in these terms, however, art does not exist for its own sake. Toward the end of *The Third Violet*, Crane did give art a fair amount of autonomy, however. As Billie returns to his New York studio and stares at the two violets Grace has presented to him, his paintings take on a life of their own: 'Upon the walls of the studio, various labors of his life in heavy gilt frames contemplated him and the violets' (*W* iii. 71). Here, art assumes the role of jealous lover. Billie's artworks compete with the violets – emblems of his love for Grace – for Billie's attention. As a lover, art is much less fickle and much more controllable. Unlike Grace, art can be enclosed – that is, contained within the boundaries of a frame. Placing Billie's paintings within gilt frames, Crane establishes a link between his creative work and his commercial artwork. An ornately gilt frame does as much to identify its contents as does a tomato can label. The gilt frames that enclose Billie's paintings offer a good contrast for the ambiguity of the final encounter between Billie and Grace in *The Third Violet*. A can of tomatoes can be wrapped with a label, and a painting can be enclosed within a frame; the love story, however, must go without closure.

6

War Dispatches

Stephen Crane's authorship of *The Red Badge of Courage* and *The Little Regiment* gave him the credentials to write about war, and his personal drive to see war with his own eyes prompted him to seek experience as a war correspondent. In March 1897 he signed a contract with William Randolph Hearst's *New York Journal* to report the impending Graeco-Turkish War. Subsequently he negotiated contracts with the S. S. McClure syndicate, which would distribute his dispatches across the United States, and also with the well-respected British daily, *The Westminster Gazette*. The quality of Crane's prose in these war dispatches rises well above contemporary journalistic standards and, in terms of literary quality, greatly exceeds *Active Service*, Crane's quasi-romantic novel inspired by his experience during the war. Though *Active Service* is not without its enthusiasts – Carl Van Doren found that 'the book glitters with impressionistic phrases' (*Work*, iv. xiv) – it is generally recognized as one of Crane's least effective works. In terms of both style and insight, Crane's best war correspondence, on the other hand, approaches the level of prose in *Red Badge*. As Michael Robertson has noted in his fine study of Crane's newspaper writing, *Stephen Crane, Journalism, and the Making of Modern American Literature*, Crane differed from contemporary novelists William Dean Howells and Henry James, both of whom disdained newspaper contributions as something well below the novel. Crane, alternatively, recognized that journalism could be approached as serious literature.

Contemporary readers understood that what Crane's war dispatches lacked as information they more than made up for in literary value. 'A Fragment of Velestino', one of the contributions he made to the *Westminster Gazette*, was delayed in the mails. By the time it reached the office of the *Gazette*, the war had ended with Greece's ignominious defeat, so the news Crane was reporting was already some weeks old. Though its informational value had been superseded by more recent reports, Crane's dispatch retained its value as literature. A note the *Gazette* editor appended to the article explains: 'Mr Stephen Crane's letters have by some accident been considerably delayed in transmission, but we make no apology for publishing them three weeks after the events to which they relate, since their literary interest, as impressions of the battlefield, are in no way diminished by the lapse of time' (*W* ix. 450–51).

The political history of Greece over the course of the nineteenth century is a stormy one. Suffice it to say that, when the century began, Greece remained under Turkish control as a part of the Ottoman empire, but by its closing decade, Greece had wrested a fair amount of autonomy from Turkey, though, in so doing, it had incurred significant political indebtedness to the European powers. As the 1890s progressed, Greece began to flex its political muscles and sought control of Crete and Macedonia. After the attack of paramilitary Greek forces on Turkish posts in Macedonia, war seemed inevitable. Crane, among dozens of other war correspondents, made his way to Greece to report the anticipated war. Velestino formed one of the key battlegrounds, and 'A Fragment of Velestino' constitutes one of Crane's finest pieces of non-fiction prose.

Much as he did in his best fiction, Crane begins this essay by capturing both the atmosphere and setting, the colour of the sky and the distance of the hills: 'The sky was of a fair and quiet blue. In the radiantly bright atmosphere of the morning the distances among the hills were puzzling in the extreme' (*W* ix. 27). Robertson has compared this opening to the start of *Red Badge*. Both place 'warfare within the setting of a serene and indifferent nature'.[1] Making the appearance of the landscape seem puzzling, Crane denotes that what he sees is alien to him, an idea he clarifies in ensuing sentences: 'The Westerner could reflect that after all his eye was accustomed to using a tree as a standard of measure, but here there were no trees. The great bold hills were naked. The landscape was indeed one which we would understand as being Biblical. A tall lean shepherd was necessary to it' (*W* ix. 27–8). Capturing the paradoxical viewpoint of someone familiar with the Bible yet unfamiliar with the East, Crane establishes an opposition between East and West. As Occidental man strives to make sense of the unfamiliar, he makes use of his only source of knowledge about the East, the Bible, a source that proves sorely inadequate for the task at hand.

Creating his landscape, Crane develops what becomes a kind of verbal postcard. The town of Volo appears in the distance, one part located on the plain adjacent to the sea and the other part 'fastened to the side of an enormous mountain. Tiny house appears above tiny house, and streets can be seen from end to end. In fact, the mountain side is so steep that the entire town there is displayed as if one looked at a lithograph. One can only dream of the view of the blue gulf there to be obtained, and of the soft splendor of the fall of evening' (*W* ix. 28). Crane's simile unmasks his design. During the war the lithograph served as a popular news medium in Greece. As Crane observes in a subsequent dispatch, 'A Portrait of Smolenski': 'There are no illustrated papers in Greece but the war has developed a great and breathless movement in lithographs' (*W* ix. 72). Basically, Crane was giving his contemporary Anglo-American readers a verbal equivalent of the lithograph and, in so doing, letting distant readers share the experience of being there.

In the third paragraph, he shifts from long shot to close-up as he describes a soldier walking away from the front. The image of the soldier's face is reminiscent of *Red Badge* in both its poignancy and its pathos: 'A great piece of white linen was wound around under his jaw, and finally tied at the top of his head in a great knot like the one grandma ties when she remedies her boy's toothache' (*W* ix. 28). Crane considers this wounded soldier's appearance, reflecting on it at length and trying to come to grips with the reason why the wounded man was walking to the hospital instead of taking the train with the other wounded. The man must have been behaving from pure instinct, he conjectures, an idea he emphasizes with a comparison: 'A rabbit when it is hurt does not wait for a train – it crawls away immediately into the bushes; and so this man had started for Volo' (*W* ix. 29).

Slowly working his way into his description of the battle, Crane presents his details in a careful order. Obviously he would have heard the gunfire well before the wounded soldier would have caught his attention, yet he withholds the noise of battle until after he has described setting and soldier. As Crane tells the story, the sound of battle occurs behind the retreating soldier. To Crane's ears, the noise of the battle is 'the roar and rumble of an enormous factory', and the wounded soldier is its 'product, not so well finished as some, but sufficient to express the plan of the machine. This wounded soldier explained the distant roar. He defined it. This – this and worse – was what was going on. This explained the meaning of all that racket. Gazing at this soldier with his awful face, one felt a new respect for the din' (*W* ix. 29). It has become commonplace to refer to everything that goes into waging war – arms and artillery, infrastructure and infantry – as a war machine. Crane takes the figurative comparison one step further as he sees what the machine produces. Ironically, this machine creates destruction.

Multiple times in 'A Fragment of Velestino' Crane reveals additional ironies as he juxtaposes the presence of war with places of peace. Consider his poignant description of a Velestino mosque:

> There was a mosque and minaret – evidences of a former Turkish occupation – near the foot of the hill. A little square faced the mosque, and there was a pool, a still and lovely pool. On its mirror-like surface it reflected part of the old dome of the mosque, and reproduced completely the round and pointed little minaret. Some cattle, deserted probably by their owner, came quietly down to the pool to drink. The sky was blue. A gentle wind rustled the foliage over a garden wall. To be sure, there was a soldier nursing a sore foot under the porch of the mosque, but even with him this scene in the angle formed by two lines of battle was eminently peace. And yet there was a curious sound in the square – spit – spit – spit; and with this sound a long tenor humming. Little clouds of dust flew from the roadway. Spit – spit. The little square, by baleful chance, had fallen under fire. Some Turks were firing at another thing, and consequently they were hitting this square. Spit – spit – spit. The cattle drank, gratefully rolling their fine and melancholy eyes. They were up to their knees in the cool water,

> and the pool reflected their stout dun-coloured bodies. By strange chance they walked into the pool at a place which caused the mosque to be between them and the line of fire. They lazily swished their long tails, and as for this spitting and kicking of dust within ten yards of them, it was as if it were not happening. (*W* ix. 32)

The presence of this mosque calls to mind the days of the Ottoman empire. In the course of Crane's description the mosque is infiltrated three times over: by cattle, a foot-weary Greek soldier, and Turkish gunfire. Crane subtly parallels the soldier and the cattle. Much as the cattle visit the reflecting pool for refreshment, the soldier seeks the mosque as a convenient place to nurse his foot. Neither convey an awareness of the mosque's cultural significance or symbolic value, yet their presence does not disturb the solemnity of the place. Similarly the onset of gunfire scarcely affects the mosque's solemnity. The cattle hardly seem threatened by the gunfire. They merely drift into the reflecting pool and, protected from the gunfire by the mosque, continue their refreshment.

Later in 'A Fragment of Velestino', Crane included a little vignette depicting Greek soldiers at their devotions that serves as a companion piece to the description of the mosque. The scene takes place at the site of a wayside shrine:

> There was a small stone shrine at the side of the trail. It contained a little holy picture of a saint, a little chromo in red and green, with a frame of gilt paper. Under this picture was a little lamp, wherein oil was sometimes burned. It was the common wayside shrine of the Greek Church. The soldiers had been marched a long way. Their faces were warm with sweat. Their blanket-rolls lay heavily upon their shoulders. Their haversacks knocked awkwardly upon their tired hips. Their rifles and double rows of long Gras cartridges must have each appeared weighty enough to sink a yacht. Moreover, many of the men still wore their thick winter overcoats, as is rather a custom among Greek soldiers, no matter how warm may be the Oriental sunshine.
>
> This weary column reached the little shrine, which was less than three hundred yards from the advanced firing line. The men at the front crossed themselves and prayed. As file after file passed, the men crossed themselves and prayed. Suddenly a great hooting shell struck the base of the shrine and lifted the structure in the air. It fell with a ringing smash, demolished. There was a spectacle of

> the nearest men scurrying in every direction to escape the flying stones, and as they ran the fingers of many of them were still at their chests as they had been when making the sign of the cross before the coming of the shell. The men in the rear of the column, finding no shrine, prayed quietly facing its ruins. (*W* ix. 36).

Unlike the mosque, which seems to endure gunfire yet remain unscathed, the shrine is obliterated by a mortar shell. Though the shrine itself is destroyed, its symbolic meaning endures, and the Christian soldier continue to practise his devotions regardless.

Crane ended 'A Fragment of Velestino' on a quiet note, blending soft music with subdued yet nevertheless colourful imagery. Some mountain shepherds who had volunteered to fight, yet who remained cloaked in their local woollens, softly sing 'the wild minor ballads of their hills. As the evening deepened', Crane continues in this, his closing paragraph, 'many men curled in their blankets and slept, but these grey-cloaked mountaineers continued to sing. Ultimately the rays of the moon outlined their figures in silver light, and it was not infrequently that shells from the persistent Turco-German batteries threw a sudden red colour on their curious garb and on the banner of their village which hung above them. They sang of war, and their songs were new to the sense, reflecting the centuries of their singing, and as the ultimate quiet of night came to the height this low chanting was the only sound. This ended one day at Velestino' (*W* ix. 44). This last sentence, which ends 'A Fragment of Velestino', is a masterpiece of understatement. Crane may have been only describing one day, yet, in so doing, he had managed to encompass the clash between East and West, Muslim and Christian, war and peace.

The Graeco-Turkish War constituted one episode in a larger political issue known as the Eastern question, which basically involved the aftermath of the Ottoman empire. The West's apparent inability to understand the East greatly complicated the issue. In a dispatch entitled 'Greek War Correspondents', Crane describes several fellow newspapermen in Greece, paying particular attention to his British colleagues, who assumed themselves to be among the few who understood the Eastern question. Generally speaking, Crane observes that the

British correspondent 'has an iron-clad and immovable way of understanding a question which reminds one unmistakably of a god. He is perfectly simple and ingenuous about it. Apparently this ability to understand the Eastern question is given him because he is a British subject. He does not state this fact, but upon looking him over, one can see no other reason for his believing that he understands the Eastern question. He appropriates a knowledge of the Eastern question as blandly as his government appropriates an island or a tribe of negroes' (*W* ix. 16). Knowledge of a native people's way of life, Crane sardonically suggests, comes with the territory.

Though the British correspondents may not have understood the Eastern question as well as they thought they did, there was one correspondent present during the Graeco-Turkish War who did have a good grasp of the issue. Stephen Crane wrote a lengthy essay on the subject. Written around the same time as his other war correspondence, the essay remained unpublished and untitled in his lifetime, but Crane's posthumous editors have assigned it the title 'The Eastern Question'. In the essay, Crane notices how Western notions of diplomacy differ markedly from Eastern ones. Whereas the Europeans see diplomacy as a 'high art', the Muslim Turks see it as a matter of 'lies and procrastination' (*W* ix. 76). Crane has much to say about the Concert of Europe, an association of the five major powers – Great Britain, France, Russia, Prussia, and Austria – dedicated to European territorial settlement, and its attitude toward Turkey. Having sided with Greece, the Concert of Europe has suddenly found itself on the losing side of the war. The Concert, which often resorted to bullying its enemies and neighbours, now must face the knowledge that it had lost:

> One could hardly have the temerity to observe the emotions of this gigantic creature, the Concert, at this particular hour. It would be an intrusion too grievous. Nor would one dare to scan the colossal countenance, broken with surprise and pain. It no doubt feels itself to be an immense and hideous bit of nonsense. It went into a thing with a great deal of solemnity and with all sorts of kow-towing and salaaming on all sides and with a loud declaration to do its own will in a certain matter and there rose up from the dark East a little man in a red fez who took it by the hair and mopped the world with it. (*W* ix. 79–80).

Crane further contrasted Europe and the East in an essay entitled 'The Turkish Army'. The draft of this essay exists in a fragmentary state, and Crane apparently never completed it. Brief as it is, the work contains several poignant insights. Turkey's success, Crane observes, fuelled a general desire among Muslims for war: 'But it is now apparent that if anyone is strolling around Europe looking for a fight he can get it from the Moslem whose late victories from inferior Greece have stirred not only his military spirit, but more than that have fired anew his religious zeal which now flames up to the sky' (*W* ix. 80). The Concert had greatly underestimated the power of the Turkish army and was consequently unprepared for the Turks' capacity to withstand hardship:

> In Athens, or for that matter in London, before the war everyone understood that the Turkish army was about as disreputable and ragged an aggregation as could be assembled in any part of the world. The Greek Prime Minister informed the newspapers that the Turkish shells could not by any chance go off. They had no regular commissionary department, their infantry ammunition was defective and scarce, and the men were in tatters and howling for the back pay which had been due the army for several centuries.
>
> It is now quite apparent that these statements are not true. But the main point is that the Turks did not mind this condition at all. There is very little in this world that the Turks do mind if they are upon a business which can be presented to them as an excursion to advance the banners of their religion. (*W* ix 80–1)

Recall the comment appended to 'A Fragment of Velestino' when it originally appeared in the *Westminster Gazette*. Crane's impressions of war between the West and the East remain in no way diminished by the lapse of time.

7

Point of View and the Short Story

In 'Crane at Velestino', another dispatch from the Graeco-Turkish War, Stephen Crane relates how the sound of war impressed him. To the author of *The Red Badge of Courage* the tremendous noise of musketry takes on an aura of beauty the first time he hears it. After conveying this impression in his dispatch, Crane appears to be having second thoughts and notes the possibility of perceiving the battle differently. He observes: 'This is one point of view. Another might be taken from the men who died there' (*W* ix. 20). Studying his representations of war, Giorgio Mariani was struck by how Crane conveyed the idea of an alternate point of view to such an extent that he used this passage from 'Crane at Velestino' to conclude his monograph *Spectacular Narratives*. By suggesting the point of view of the dead, Crane, according to Mariani, reminds readers of the impossibility of such a perspective.

In his reportage Crane may have been able to imply alternate points of view, yet he was fundamentally restricted to his own. Within his imaginative writings, however, he had much greater opportunity to experiment with point of view. Though he usually wrote his novels and short stories from the third person, he often focalized the point of view from the perspective of one of his characters. *The Red Badge of Courage*, for instance, is narrated in the third person but is frequently focalized from Henry Fleming's perspective. Crane's diction parallels his use of perspective. In *Red Badge*, the third-person narrator frequently co-opts language Henry is likely to use. Crane's short stories further develop the relationship between point of view and diction and offer the opportunity to scrutinize his unique style.

'A Man and Some Others', less frequently studied nowadays than Crane's other major tales, was greatly admired at the time of its initial appearance. Joseph Conrad, for one, called the story 'immense' and preferred it over 'The Open Boat'. Conrad did not delineate precisely why the story so impressed him other than to characterize its appeal in an exclamation to Crane: 'Confound you – you fill the blamed landscape'.[1] Conrad's remark is a little cryptic: the landscape Crane depicts in 'A Man and Some Others' is quite stark. What fills it, however, is Crane's multifaceted gaze.

The story begins with the following paragraph:

> Dark mesquit spread from horizon to horizon. There was no house or horseman from which a mind could evolve a city or a crowd. The world was declared to be a desert and unpeopled. Sometimes, however, on days when no heat-mist arose, a blue shape, dim, of the substance of a specter's veil, appeared in the southwest, and a pondering sheep-herder might remember that there were mountains. (*W* v. 53)

The initial sentence of this passage describes a vast, desolate landscape; the second prompts the reader to imagine what may exist beyond his field of vision, yet simultaneously conveys the impossibility of so doing. The third, written in the passive voice, gives its readers a solipsistic conclusion: the world and the individual field of vision are co-terminous. The fourth and last sentence, however, introduces a privileged perspective, that of 'a pondering sheep-herder', someone who possesses imagination, memory, and a familiarity with the landscape, who can, on a clear day, see vague shapes at the edge of the horizon.

Bill, the man of the title, is introduced before two more paragraphs pass. He, like the 'pondering sheep-herder', possesses a privileged gaze: he discerns a Mexican sheepherder approaching from the distance like a ghost. When the Mexican comes within earshot, he orders Bill off the land. Bill refuses to budge.

Technically speaking, Crane's point of view in 'A Man and Some Others' is omniscient, third-person, but occasionally the narrative is focalized from Bill's perspective. The narrator seems to be looking out from behind Bill's eyes. Before long Crane introduces another pair of eyes, those of a naive young stranger who arrives on horseback yet sits uneasily in the saddle. The stranger's initial impressions are articulated as part of the dialogue, yet once he enters the story, the narrative focalization sometimes shifts from Bill to the stranger. Bill soon kills one of the Mexican sheepherders, while the stranger looks on helplessly. The stranger resolves to leave, but when his horse flees 'in the uncanny death run known to men who have seen the finish of brave horses' (*W* v. 64), he is forced to witness and even to participate in the ensuing carnage.

During the firefight, Bill is mortally wounded, and the young stranger must kill one of the Mexican sheepherders in self-defence. After Bill has expired and the surviving Mexicans have fled, the stranger eventually leaves the scene as 'the bushes, nodding and whispering, their leaf-faces turned toward the scene behind him, swung and swung again into stillness and the peace of the wilderness' (*W* v. 67). Heading away, the stranger turns his back to the scene, but Crane shifts perspective again. Through the use of personification, he lets the mesquite bushes serve as final witness.

Many consider 'The Blue Hotel' Stephen Crane's finest short story. H. L. Mencken went even further in his praise, calling it not only Crane's finest, but also the finest of any author. In Mencken's words, 'The Blue Hotel' is 'superlative among short stories' (*Work*, x. xii). Crane's narrative strategy in 'The Blue Hotel' differs significantly from that of 'A Man and Some Others'. Though narrated in the third person, the tale is rarely focalized from the characters' perspective and seldom incorporates their characteristic diction as part of the narrative. Since Crane had decided to tell much of the story in dialogue, he recognized that it would be better to maintain a consistent voice in his narration and let the voices of his characters distinguish themselves in the dialogue. To that end, he adapted a fairly traditional narrative stance, that of a detached, yet witty and urbane, third-person observer.

The landscape of 'The Blue Hotel' is scarcely less harsh and desolate than that of 'A Man and Some Others', yet the story begins with a comparison that emphasizes the cleverness of the narrator over the starkness of the environment: 'The Palace

Hotel at Fort Romper was painted a light blue, a shade that is on the legs of a kind of heron, causing the bird to declare its position against any background. The Palace Hotel, then, was always screaming and howling in a way that made the dazzling winter landscape of Nebraska seem only a gray swampish hush' (*W* v. 142). This and other clever descriptions on the narrator's part are, by and large, beyond the capacity of the story's characters, whom the narrator proceeds to introduce as he begins establishing plot. Hotel proprietor Pat Scully has convinced three travellers – an Easterner, a cowboy, and a Swede – to patronize the Palace Hotel. Once inside, their personalities begin to emerge, and, with the introduction of Johnnie, the tension begins to rise.

The urbanity of the narrator's voice lets the dialogue stand out in contrast, but the characters' speeches reveal the influence of the written word. Their diction and their rhetoric seem borrowed from the cheap print culture. Early in the story Scully speaks like a promotional pamphlet published by the Fort Romper Chamber of Commerce. 'Why, man', Scully tells the Swede, 'we're goin' to have a line of ilictric street-cars in this town next spring. . . . there's a new railroad goin' to be built down from Broken Arm to here. Not to mintion the four churches and the smashin' big brick school-house. Then there's the big factory, too. Why, in two years Romper'll be a met-tro-*pol*-is' (*W* v. 149–50). Elsewhere, Scully's words reflect the cheap press in other ways. As the narrator explains, 'Scully's speech was always a combination of Irish brogue and idiom, Western twang and idiom, and scraps of curiously formal diction taken from the story-books and newspapers' (*W* v. 154). The Swede, in turn, has been heavily influenced by cheap novels set in the Wild West. As the Easterner observes, he seems to have been 'reading dime-novels, and he thinks he's right out in the middle of it – the shootin' and stabbin' and all' (*W* v. 152). The relationship is reciprocal: dialogue is embedded in Crane's printed tale; the printed word is embedded in his characters' speech. Man is made of malleable stuff: what he reads makes an impression on how he thinks, speaks, and acts.

The Easterner, too, is shaped by what he encounters. His name makes this idea abundantly clear: Mr Blanc. The name recalls Locke's notion of the mind as a *tabula rasa*, yet Crane updates Locke by changing his figurative comparison from a written to a visual medium. After the Swede has accused Johnnie of cheating at cards, and they go out into the snow to fight, the others come along to bear witness:

> During this pause, the Easterner's mind, like a film, took lasting impressions of three men – the iron-nerved master of the ceremony; the Swede, pale, motionless, terrible; and Johnnie, serene yet ferocious, brutish yet heroic. The entire prelude had in it a tragedy greater than the tragedy of action, and this aspect was accentuated by the long mellow cry of the blizzard, as it sped the tumbling and wailing flakes into the black abyss of the south. (*W* v. 159).

Writing 'The Blue Hotel' after motion pictures had emerged as a form of commercial entertainment, Crane makes explicit what he had anticipated in *Red Badge*. Comparing the Easterner's mind to a film negative, Crane emphasizes how easily what we see influences who we are.

After the fight, the Swede enters a saloon, gets drunk, and picks a fight with a gambler, who stabs and kills him. 'The Blue Hotel' ends some months later when the Easterner and the cowboy happen to meet. The Easterner tells the cowboy that the Swede was right: Johnnie had been cheating. The Easterner confesses the shame he felt for not admitting Johnnie's deceit at the time: 'Johnnie was cheating. I saw him. I know it. I saw him. And I refused to stand up and be a man. I let the Swede fight it out alone. And you – you were simply puffing around the place and wanting to fight. And then old Scully himself! We are all in it! This poor gambler isn't even a noun. He is kind of an adverb. Every sin is the result of a collaboration. We, five of us, have collaborated in the murder of this Swede' (*W* v. 170). Equating people with parts of speech, the Easterner's words reinforce the proximity of word and deed. Traditionally, narrative involves a process of converting behaviour into words as a way of making a series of events comprehensible. As various parts of speech come together to form a sentence, these individual men have come together to form an unwitting collaboration. Each man's behaviour makes an indelible impression on every other man he contacts and their subsequent actions after the moment of contact cannot be extricated from the whole course of action.

In *Green Hills of Africa*, Ernest Hemingway lauded 'The Blue Hotel' and 'The Open Boat' as Crane's two finest short stories. H. G. Wells went even further in his appreciation of 'The Open Boat', calling the story 'beyond all question, the crown of all his work' (*CH* 271). The tale is based on a life-threatening personal experience. Having made several unsuccessful attempts to reach Cuba in 1897, where he hoped to cover the Cuban revolution, Crane ultimately obtained passage aboard the *Commodore*. When the ship foundered and sank, Crane escaped in a lifeboat and, after a harrowing experience at sea, made it safely to land. 'The Open Boat' came as an afterthought. Crane initially wrote up the adventure as a newspaper report, which was published under the title, 'Stephen Crane's Own Story'.

Telling the story of his own experiences in an open boat in the form of a personal account, Crane had little choice in the matter but to tell it in the first person, yet even this point of view he seems reluctant to accept. The report begins by describing the appearance of the *Commodore* at the dock in Jacksonville prior to its departure. Though Crane would sail aboard the vessel, it is unclear over the course of the first several paragraphs whether he is aboard or simply reporting its departure from shore. Not until the *Commodore* pulls away from the dock and blasts its whistle does it become clear that Crane is aboard and headed to sea.

Crane knew the thrilling experience gave him the stuff for a fine short story, and he later recast his adventure as 'The Open Boat'. Significantly, Crane changed the narrative point of view in the transfer from truth to fiction. The first person of 'Stephen Crane's Own Story' gives way to an omniscient, third-person narrative, and 'The Open Boat' begins after the ship has foundered and the survivors have made it into the lifeboat, where they have been for some time. Though 'Stephen Crane's Own Story' begins with an obvious reluctance to admit its point of view, 'The Open Boat' flaunts its third-person, omniscient narrator from its first paragraph, indeed, its first sentence:

> None of them knew the colour of the sky. Their eyes glanced level, and were fastened upon the waves that swept toward them. These waves were of the hue of slate, save for the tops, which were of

> foaming white, and all of the men knew the colours of the sea. The horizon narrowed and widened, and dipped and rose, and at all times its edge was jagged with waves that seemed thrust up in points like rocks. (*W* v. 68)

With no formalities, the narrator insinuates himself into the heads of all of the characters in the lifeboat. He knows what each knows and sees what they see.

The narrator reaches such a level of familiarity with the conditions inside the lifeboat that it seems as if he were in it: 'By the very last star of truth, it is easier to steal eggs from under a hen than it was to change seats in the dingey' (*W* v. 72). The narrator is apparently borrowing his diction from one of the men in the boat, yet it is unclear whose words he is voicing. A few paragraphs after this passage, the narrator achieves an extraordinary distance from the boat as he almost seems to peer at it from on high: 'She seemed just a wee thing wallowing, miraculously, top-up, at the mercy of five oceans' (*W* v. 73).

Elsewhere, the narrator achieves distance from the men in the boat by revealing that he knows more than they do. As the tired and desperate men make speculations regarding the possibility of a life-saving station being near by, the narrator states, 'It is fair to say here that there was not a life-saving station within twenty miles in either direction, but the men did not know this fact and in consequence they made dark and opprobrious remarks concerning the eyesight of the nation's life-savers' (*W* v. 76). Here, the reader may take issue with this remark, which does seem unfair. Withholding the absence of life-saving stations, the narrator reveals how futile the hopes of these men are. Consequently, they seem foolish for their ignorance.

Though the narrator seems to have the ability to enter his characters' minds and read their thoughts, he does not always take full advantage of this ability. Sometimes he prefers to articulate their thoughts himself. He observes, 'As for the reflections of the men, there was a great deal of rage in them. Perchance they might be formulated thus: "If I am going to be drowned – if I am going to be drowned – if I am going to be drowned, why, in the name of the seven mad gods who rule the sea, was I allowed to come thus far and contemplate sand and trees?" ' (*W* v. 77). Thoughts are non-verbal, Crane implies. Words that express them are, in turn, a kind of formula, an approximation of thought. Later, the narrator articulates these same thoughts, yet isolates them. They appear in inverted commas, but they are not accompanied by explanatory tag clauses. In other words, Crane refuses to remind readers that these thoughts represent the narrator's approximations, not necessarily the precise thoughts of any of the characters.

As the story progresses, the narrative becomes increasingly focalized from the correspondent's perspective, but it is careful not to attribute all formulated thoughts to him. They are the narrator's invention. The fact that both the correspondent and the narrator are projections of Crane's self only complicates matters further. Varying the narrative distance and changing the focalization, Crane, remarkably, creates a narrative that discursively replicates the story it tells. Narrating a story of men stranded in the vast space of the ocean, Crane strands his readers within the space of his narrative, disorientating them as he tosses them to and fro, removing traditional narrative moorings and letting them struggle toward comprehension.

8

The Monster: The Idea of Order at Whilomville

'Little Jim was, for the time, engine Number 36, and he was making the run between Syracuse and Rochester'. So begins *The Monster*, the novella Stephen Crane set in Whilomville, the fictional city he loosely based on Port Jervis, New York, where he would later set a series of short stories incorporating several of the same characters from *The Monster*. In his earlier writings, Crane had proven himself to be a master in the use of simile, yet he chose metaphor over simile to open *The Monster* and thus directly equates Jimmie Trescott and a locomotive engine, man and machine. As a locomotive, Jimmie transforms a route around the flower beds of his family's yard into an east–west route across upstate New York. Jimmy's path emphasizes how the railroad, quite literally, formed lines across the surface of the state and, indeed, the continent. The railroad was not only a means of transporting goods and people from one point to another, it was also a means of connecting those points, a way of establishing order across the land.

As the opening of *The Monster* goes, Jimmie deliberately pretends he is behind schedule. His purpose for so doing is fairly obvious: it gives him an excuse to speed as fast as he can. His ability to imagine being behind schedule, however, indicates that man's attempt to impose order on one particular natural process – the passage of time – is less than perfect. Becoming a locomotive engine himself, Jimmie makes the garden cart he pulls behind him into a train. As he swings around a flower bed a cart wheel destroys a peony. Though the railroad may impose order on the natural world, it seemingly cannot do so without harming it. Reverting from engine to boy, Jimmy anticipates punishment and looks toward his father, who is busy mowing the lawn. His back to the flower bed, Dr Trescott has not seen the accident and thus continues his gardening chores.

The doctor's particular activity reinforces the idea of imposing order on the environment, too. At its most fundamental level, lawnmowing constitutes a battle against entropy, the underlying principle of which deems that things naturally tend toward disorder. Since lawns naturally tend toward growing wild and weedy, it takes diligent effort to prevent them from so doing. So both Jimmy and his father are engaged in analogous efforts. Generally speaking, the two are inscribing the surface of the earth with lines, trying to impose order onto nature, which resists the order man imposes.

Entropy has become a defining feature of postmodern American literature, and the term, which most of us learn in chemistry class, entered the literary discourse with the publication of the minor postmodernist classic, Thomas Pynchon's short story 'Entropy' (1960). The idea predates postmodernism, of course, and authors long before Pynchon made use of it. Pynchon's story directly credits his literary antecedent, Henry Adams, whose autobiography, *The Education of Henry Adams*, devoted much attention to contrasting the chaos of nature with man's dream of order. In 'Entropy', Callisto has created a controlled environment and hermetically sealed himself inside his Washington, DC, flat one winter, where he remains with his girlfriend Aubade. In the flat beneath a chaotic party continues while outdoors the temperature seems to remain a constant thirty-seven degrees Fahrenheit, which, though not too unusual for February in DC, Callisto understands as an omen of apocalypse. Before Pynchon, few literary works had incorporated the notion of entropy in more dramatic fashion than *The Monster*, which is more often interpreted in social terms than physical ones. In the first part of *The Monster*, Crane develops several images regarding the theme of order. In the second part – that is, after fire destroys the Trescott home and horribly disfigures Henry Johnson – subsequent attempts to impose order on the world appear inadequate.

After destroying the peony, Jimmy displays his cognizance of the order of things. He understands that he has made a mistake, feels shame, and awaits punishment at the hands of his father. When Jimmy's anticipated punishment is not immediately forthcoming, he interrupts his father's activity to confess what he has done. Dr Trescott then forbids Jimmy from playing train. Duly punished, Jimmy seeks solace in the company of his friend Henry Johnson, the family's black groom. Busy cleaning the mud from the Trescotts' buggy, Henry, too, is engaged in his own battle with entropy. Henry's presence at the Trescott home reinforces the accepted racial order in nineteenth-century Whilomville, where the black man remains subservient to the white. Henry's friendship with Jimmy exemplifies another accepted racial pattern, which American literature had incorporated before and has incorporated since yet never so well as in Mark Twain's *The Adventures of Huckleberry Finn*. Like Jim in Twain's novel, Henry Johnson is a kindly black man who befriends and mothers a troublesome boy.

Evenings, having fulfilled his responsibilities for the Trescotts, Henry dons his finest duds and goes out on the town. Though Henry, quite literally, creates a spectacle of himself and attracts the attention of all who see him walk down the street, his extravagant appearance does not necessarily violate the racial order that exists in Whilomville. The sharp-dressed black man had already become a stereotype. Conforming to the stereotype, Henry is merely fulfilling prescribed notions of behaviour.

Detailing Henry's passage through the streets of Whilomville, Crane incidentally describes the efforts the city was making to impose order on itself. The barbershop is one of the town's most prominent gathering places. In the time before safety razors, men would go to the barbershop on a daily basis to be shaved, a process that runs parallel to Dr Trescott's lawnmowing, a parallel Crane makes explicit. Describing Dr Trescott's lawnmowing in the opening scene, Crane observes, 'The doctor was shaving this lawn as if it were a priest's chin' (*W* vii. 9).

Electricity represents another obvious way order has been imposed upon the community. The lights at the street corners and the power lines above the street cars, not to mention the tracks beneath them, inscribe visible lines on the surface of the city. Though intended to brighten the streets and make night more closely resemble day, the electric lights illuminate much of Whilomville that had formerly been obscured. In one such place, they inadvertently serve to display 'a row of tumble-down houses leaning together like paralytics' (*W* vii. 15). The description suggests that the new-fangled lights, though imposing order on the city streets, emphasize the fact that entropy is an ongoing process that stops for neither day nor night. Elsewhere, the electric lights, instead of illuminating, seem merely to rearrange the night and even deepen it in places. Elaborating his description of the lighted streets, Crane mentions a policeman who seems to appear from nowhere; he comes 'suddenly from the darkness' (*W* vii. 17). If policemen can hide in the shadows, then, implicitly, so can the criminals they pursue.

As a way to protect the public and maintain civic order, fire companies began to be established in small towns and big cities across the United States during the nineteenth century. These hose companies, at their most fundamental level, also battled entropy as they sought to control the ravages of fire. They imposed further order on the city by dividing it into districts and, therefore, creating boundaries between parts of the city where none had existed before. Even as the hose companies served to impose order on the city, they gave rise to disorder, as fierce rivalries developed among the various companies and residents of each district. Crane incorporated such rivalries into *The Monster* as he mentioned the fights they prompted among the children of Whilomville: 'Feuds, which the boys forgot and remembered according to chance or the importance of some recent event, existed all through the town' (*W* vii. 27).

From the description of Henry Johnson's night on the town, *The Monster* shifts to portraying the behaviour of other people in Whilomville during their night out. Once news of the fire reaches the crowd, the people disperse almost instantly. Members of the hose companies head toward their stations, and the general public heads toward the fire, mainly for purposes of gawking. Crane's figurative description of the crowd's movement accentuates its dispersal: 'In a flash the company of indolent and cynical young men had vanished like a snowball disrupted by dynamite' (*W* vii. 18). Crane expands the traditional prepositional phrase – 'in a flash' – to suggest precisely what it means. Dynamiting a snowball vastly accelerates the natural tendency toward disorder.

Henry Johnson, in the vanguard of those approaching the fire, reaches the Trescott home and selflessly enters the burning building to rescue Jimmie, who is trapped on the second floor. Bundling Jimmie in a blanket and carrying him from his bedroom, Henry finds the front stairs blocked by the flames. Thinking quickly, he remembers the back stairs that lead to Dr Trescott's laboratory, which has an exit of its own. Henry makes it as far as the laboratory, where he collapses. Jimmy remains safe in his blanket, yet Henry, who has fallen with his face upturned toward the doctor's workbench, becomes disfigured by a corrosive liquid spilling from the bench.

Beyond the destruction it wreaks, the fire also breaks down other ways in which order had been imposed on the city. Hose companies cross over from their own districts into the district containing the Trescott home to help dowse the fire. The back alleys, which had served as boundaries demarcating class, become permeable, for 'a young man who was a brakeman on the railway, and lived in one of the rear streets near the Trescotts' enters their home to retrieve Henry's seemingly lifeless form from the laboratory (*W* vii. 26). Calamity can obliterate class distinctions.

Happily, Jimmy survives relatively unscathed. Henry's fate is less felicitous. Horribly disfigured and on the verge of death, Henry survives by the skill and care of Dr Trescott. Neighbours and friends urge the doctor to simply let nature takes its course, that is, to let Henry die, yet the doctor, refusing to turn his back on the man who saved his son's life, keeps Henry alive. The doctor's efforts are not dissimilar to his act of lawnmowing. Much as it is the homeowner's responsibility to battle entropy by regularly mowing his lawn, it is the physician's responsibility to battle nature's course and save lives whenever possible. Surviving his horrible disfigurement, Henry Johnson, like Frankenstein's monster before him, becomes a symbol of man's effort to use his knowledge to alter the course of nature.

The doctor places Henry with Alek Williams and his family and pays them generously for their hospitality, yet even they have difficulty coping when Henry is in the house. One evening the doctor's neighbour, Judge Hagenthorpe, visits Alek to hear his complaints. Alek has difficulty explaining precisely why he and his family dislike Henry's presence, yet, in a foreshadowing of the end of *The Monster*, Alek blurts out that his wife can no longer receive 'lady callahs' (*W* vii. 36).

Before long Henry escapes from the Williams family and, as he strolls Whilomville in a manner akin to his pre-conflagration promenades, he affects the city's population as the stick of dynamite affects the snowball. A local police officer, reporting Henry's effect on the residents of Watermelon Alley, observes, 'Whoo! He stampeded the whole outfit. Men, women, and children running pell-mell, and yelling. They say one old woman broke her leg, or something, shinning over a fence. Then he went right out on the main street, and an Irish girl threw a fit, and there was a sort of riot' (*W* vii. 48).

In saving Henry, Dr Trescott had used his medical skill to subvert the course of nature. Henry's survival disrupts the orderly lives of the Whilomville citizenry. Formerly they had accepted him as he fulfilled the stereotype of the negro dandy. Now, with his cruelly misshapen face, he has become a grotesque parody of his former self. The effect Henry has on the population of Whilomville reveals the hypocrisy of the social order they had formerly accepted.

Though the town is ready to have Henry shipped off to a public institution, Dr Trescott, unwilling to let others control Henry's fate, takes him in, gives him a black veil akin to the minister's in the Hawthorne tale, and, having rebuilt his home, allows Henry to groom his horses again.

By his actions, the doctor turns himself into a pariah. The townspeople want nothing to do with him, and his practice rapidly dwindles. Mrs Trescott, too, is shunned by the townsfolk. The Whilomville women still practise the tradition of reception day, the one day in the week each woman would stay home to receive visitors. One winter afternoon, on her reception day, Mrs Trescott receives only one lady caller. Crane personally saw nothing wrong with this. In 'The Stove', another of the Whilomville stories, he viciously denounced the ladies' tea party, calling it 'the result of a conspiracy of certain unenlightened people to make life still more uncomfortable' (*W* vii. 200). Other contemporary authors similarly critiqued the custom of reception day. In *The Awakening,* published the same year as *The Monster and Other Stories,* Kate Chopin has her heroine rebel against the tradition of reception day. Mrs Trescott, however, accepts the social conventions of reception day and is devastated by the snubbing she receives at the hands of Whilomville society.

As *The Monster* ends, Dr Trescott enters their home, stomps the snow from his boots, and starts looking for his wife. Before he meets her, he finds Jimmie reading 'a large book concerning giraffes and tigers and crocodiles' (*W* vii. 64). Reading a children's book of natural history, Jimmie engages in behaviour reinforcing the general theme of man's attempt to order nature.

Finding his wife in tears, the doctor learns that she has been snubbed by the community and tries to comfort her. *The Monster* ends with the following paragraph:

> The wind was whining around the house and the snow beat aslant upon the windows. Sometimes the coal in the stove settled with a crumbling sound and the four panes of mica flushed a sudden new crimson. As he sat holding her head on his shoulder, Trescott found himself occasionally trying to count the cups. There were fifteen of them. (*W* vii. 65).

Outdoors nature takes its course. The peonies are dormant and the grass need not be cut until the spring. Inside the cast-iron stove artificially heats the room. Contained by the walls of the stove, the fire burns in a controlled and orderly fashion. The many unused teacups, too, are arranged in an orderly manner. Crane's closing imagery juxtaposes the orderly interior of the newly constructed Trescott home with the fury of a New York winter outside. Whereas Aubade in Pynchon's story ultimately smashes the window separating Callisto's controlled interior from the Washington winter, the Trescotts remain separated from the outdoors. The interior world of the Trescotts is ordered yet isolated from the community.

For his biography of Crane, Thomas Beer put words in the mouth of *Century* editor Richard Watson Gilder, who supposedly rejected *The Monster* with the remark, 'We couldn't publish that thing with half the expectant mothers in America on our subscription list'. This detail, undoubtedly fabricated by Beer, continues to be quoted as fact, yet has gone largely unexplicated. Though the statement lacks biographical validity, considered as a critical comment on the story, it captures an important aspect of it. These words reflect a prevalent superstition, specifically, that the pregnant woman who sees a monster will bear a monstrous baby. The sight of Henry Johnson, even mediated through the printed word, Beer suggested, is sufficient to disrupt the natural order of things.

One contemporary reviewer said something much different regarding the idea of order the story embodied, however. Robert Bridges, in his contemporary appreciation, observed of *The Monster*: 'It is incident, action, character, in quick succession – and often apparently disjointed and irrelevant. But when the last block is put in place the whole design flashes into an orderly picture – like the landscape painted on six separate boards by a variety artist, and suddenly clapped into a gilt frame' (*CH* 258). Subsequent critics generally agree that *The Monster* is the most formally perfect work Crane composed. The resulting combination of form and content is significantly different from 'The Open Boat'. Whereas Crane chose a narrative approach that paralleled the events narrated in 'The Open Boat', *The Monster*, alternatively, is a highly ordered story that takes disorder for its subject. With *The Monster*, Stephen Crane makes order incorporate disorder.

Conclusion

Novels, short stories, sketches, war dispatches, history: Stephen Crane's literary output between the time *The Red Badge of Courage* appeared in 1895 and his death in 1900 was varied and prolific. Despite the breadth of his work during the last five years of his life, he continued to be known primarily as the author of *The Red Badge of Courage*, an epithet that usually appeared beneath his name on the title pages of his subsequent works. Though he did wish to be known as more than an author of war stories – as the tales that comprise the *Whilomville Stories* indicate – there is no evidence to suggest that Crane wished to shake his reputation as the author of *Red Badge*. The notoriety *Red Badge* had earned him had made possible much of his subsequent work – the Civil War stories that comprise *The Little Regiment*; his war correspondence from Greece and, later, Cuba and Puerto Rico; his second volume of poetry, *War Is Kind*; the tales of war published in the day's most prominent magazines and collected posthumously as *Wounds in the Rain*. In 1898, William Heinemann, Crane's British publisher, took advantage of his reputation and issued *Pictures of War*, which combined the texts of *Red Badge* and *The Little Regiment* into a single volume. During the last year of his life, Crane's reputation had allowed him to reach a fairly lucrative agreement to compose a series of articles about great battles of the past for *Lippincott's Magazine*. Researched and largely written by Kate Lyon, these accounts were gathered in the posthumous collection *Great Battles of the World*.

Since its initial appearance in 1895, *Red Badge* has remained in print, but much of Crane's other writings were neglected in the decade and a half following his death. When Peter

Somerville, a British admirer of Crane's writings and editor of the *Englishman*, wrote to Joseph Conrad in 1915 wondering whether he would be willing to contribute an article about Crane to the magazine, Conrad responded frankly: 'Believe me my dear Sir no paper, no review, would look at anything that I or anybody else could write about Crane. They would laugh at the suggestion. Crane? Who's Crane? Who cares for Crane?' Conrad continued, 'Mere literary excellence won't save a man's memory. . . . Sad but true. I hardly meet anyone now who knows or remembers anything of him. For the younger oncoming writers he does not exist, simply. One or two have heard of the Red Badge and asked me "What sort of thing it is" '.[1]

Conrad overgeneralized: there was a modicum of interest in Crane's work in Great Britain at the time. That same year, Heinemann reissued two Crane titles: *George's Mother*, which appeared as part of the series Heinemann's Sevenpenny Novels, and *Maggie*, which was reissued again three years later as part of the series Heinemann's Cheaper Novels. Of course Heinemann may have reissued these works simply to expand his list of cheap reprints with titles to which he already held the rights. The reissue of another Crane title around this same time, however, was more purposeful. In 1916, Heinemann reissued *The Little Regiment* in a cheap edition under the title *Pictures of War*. This timely reissue sought to capitalize on the fervour generated by World War I. With the onset of war, a new generation found relevance in Crane's work.

Another Crane title also appeared during the war: in 1914 the London firm of Hodder and Stoughton reissued *Great Battles of the World* as part of the series The Daily Telegraph War Books. The series was intended primarily for officers and soldiers at the front. Some titles provided practical, up-to-date advice concerning military logistics and intelligence. Others recounted battles that had taken place in recent months. Yet others, like the Crane volume, retold classic battles from military history. Altogether the books served to inform as well as to motivate British soldiers on the front. Though Crane had little hand in drafting the account of great battles that bears his name, this wartime edition of *Great Battles of the World* takes on importance in the history of Crane's critical reception. War helped readers recognize the value of Crane's work.

World War II renewed interest in Crane. In 1939, the year France declared war on Germany, a French edition of *Red Badge, La Conquête du courage: Épisode de la Guerre de Sécession*, appeared. Great Britain also declared war on Germany in 1939, and a new British edition of *Red Badge* appeared that year as part of the popular series Collins Pocket Classics. After the United States entered the war, *Red Badge* appeared in several cheap paperback editions. The first Pocket Books edition appeared in 1942; so did the first Washington Square Press edition and the first Penguin edition. Also that year Ernest Hemingway published *Men at War*, his beefy anthology that included short stories, excerpts from novels, and the complete first-edition text of *Red Badge*, which, in Hemingway's words, is 'one of the finest books of our literature'.

The popularity of *Red Badge* during World War II helped solidify Crane's literary reputation, and after the war numerous editions of this and other works appeared, many intended for use in junior high, high school, and college classrooms. *Red Badge* was translated into many languages during the 1950s, including Croatian, German, Greek, Hungarian, Italian, Portuguese, and Russian. Subsequent wars have continued to perpetuate Crane's recognition, but there have been so many new editions of *Red Badge* published since World War II that it is difficult to discern which new editions may have been prompted directly by war. Still, some editions stand out. Examining a checklist of translations, one cannot help but notice *Trong khói lu'*, the first Vietnamese translation, published in Saigon in 1966.

Of the numerous editions published in English since World War II, two seem particularly notable, one in the 1950s and another in the late 1970s. *The Red Badge of Courage and Other Stories* (1957), edited by Daniel Hoffman as part of the series Harper's Modern Classics, is remarkable, not for its text of *Red Badge*, but for Hoffman's curious selection of short works to accompany the novel. Instead of including those short stories widely considered Crane's best – 'The Blue Hotel', 'A Man and Some Others', 'The Open Boat' – Hoffman included five short works in the following order: 'The Veteran', 'A Mystery of Heroism', 'An Episode of War', 'Ouida's Masterpiece', and 'The Gratitude of a Nation'.

Hoffman's inclusion of 'The Veteran' is not unusual. Other anthologists before had grouped the story with *Red Badge*. Both, after all, shared the same protagonist, and 'The Veteran' can be, and has been understood as an epilogue to Crane's war novel. Hoffman's inclusion of 'A Mystery of Heroism' and 'An Episode of War' also makes good sense. Both are tales of the Civil War, and many readers consider them Crane's two finest short stories of war. Like *Red Badge*, the two are tinged with irony. Both lack the ambiguous attitude toward courage present in *Red Badge*, however. Including these instead of Crane's tales of adventure, Hoffman reinforced his reputation as primarily an author of war stories. Overall, Hoffman appears less interested in showing the diversity of Crane's oeuvre and more interested in showing the diversity of Crane's attitude toward courage.

Hoffman interprets *Red Badge* as an ironic portrayal of courage. The insightful introduction to his edition, combined with his careful selection of complementary works, softens the impact of Crane's irony. Introducing the edition, Hoffman observes, 'In *The Red Badge of Courage* Crane's view of courage – of Henry's courage, that is – is so ironical that we may not at once perceive his mystical valuation of true courage, when it occurs'.[2] Though a shrewd reader of Crane's work, Hoffman was also a decorated war veteran. He had served in the US Army Air Force for three years during World War II and was awarded the Legion of Merit. Recognizing Crane's irony in *Red Badge*, Hoffman simply could not let the work stand as Crane's only depiction of courage.

The two short, non-fiction works with which Hoffman ended the edition elaborate upon Crane's general attitude toward courage. 'Ouida's Masterpiece', a review of *Under Two Flags* by the popular novelist, is Crane's only known piece of literary criticism, and it is good enough to make us regret he did not write more. Crane's admiration for a colourful character named Cigarette indicates his own conception of Henry Fleming: 'She never intended Cigarette to be splendid, and perhaps this is why the girl appears to some of us as really the best character in the book. She is a figure of flesh among all these painted gods. She has imperfections, thank heaven, and it is very nice to come upon a good, sound imperfection when one has grown surfeited with the company of gods'. In his concluding paragraph Crane characterizes *Under Two Flags* as 'a song of the brave' and asserts that the novel voices 'the old spirit of dauntless deed and sacrifice which is the soul of literature in every age'.[3]

'The Gratitude of a Nation', an unpublished essay Hoffman found among Crane's papers while doing research for his fine critical study of Crane's verse, *The Poetry of Stephen Crane*, was originally written as an occasional piece for Decoration Day. Written about the same time as *Red Badge*, 'The Gratitude of a Nation' exalts courage without irony. In the future, Crane observes, authors will 'strive to royally celebrate the deeds of the brave, simple, quiet men who crowded upon the opposing bayonets of their country's enemies'. The departed soldiers, however, will be unaware of the appreciation of their countrymen, so Crane tells his readers, 'Let us watch with apprehension this departure of an army, one by one, one by one. Let the last words that they hear from us be words of gratitude and affection'.[4] Making 'The Gratitude of a Nation' a coda to his edition of *Red Badge*, Hoffman allows Crane's ironic war novel to end with a paean to the brave soldier.

Perhaps no edition of *Red Badge* published since World War II has been more important than the one prepared by Henry Binder from Crane's surviving manuscript. Binder originally completed the edition as his doctoral dissertation at the University of Southern California under the direction of Hershel Parker, who relates the history of the edition in *Flawed Texts and Verbal Icons*. According to Parker, Binder's edition solves the prevailing critical controversy surrounding *Red Badge*, for it shows that what some critics have seen as Crane's intentional ambiguity actually resulted from changes Crane's editor and publisher imposed on him. *Red Badge*, Parker explains, is not 'a maturation story but instead is an ironic story in which an egotistical kid gets away with desertion and at the end is so gleeful that no one caught him that he has no time for compassion for a fallen comrade'.[5]

The critical controversy regarding Henry Fleming's maturity has persisted because, in Parker's view, those advocating Crane's ambiguity – predominantly academics associated with the New Criticism – failed to examine the textual evidence.

While the same accusation can be justifiably levelled at much of the New Critical practice, the case of *Red Badge* is more complex simply because of the novel's subject matter – war. If Crane wrote a tale of an egotistical kid who gets away with desertion, then it is no wonder his contemporary editor imposed changes on its text. Many veterans remained alive and occupied places of prominence in community and society. The books about the war that were being written at the time were mainly romanticized regimental histories. The thoroughly ironic depiction of war apparent in Crane's original manuscript text was unacceptable to contemporaries. Crane's irony remained unacceptable to readers after World War II, as Hoffman's edition suggests. The Binder edition, which restores Crane's first complete text, while reflecting his original intentions, is also a product of the post-Vietnam war era. In other words, not until Vietnam could Crane's ironic text achieve any degree of acceptance.

Now, a quarter-century after Binder completed his dissertation, a new war and, consequently, a new era has begun. Widespread contempt for war has been replaced with newfound respect for heroism and courage. Since it first appeared in 1895, the interpretation of *The Red Badge of Courage* has shifted as attitudes toward war have changed, yet the novel has endured. Few authors before or since Stephen Crane have so universally captured the experience of war.

Notes

CHAPTER 1. SULLIVAN COUNTY SKETCHES

1. Milne Holton, *Cylinder of Vision: The Fiction and Journalistic Writing of Stephen Crane* (Baton Rouge: Louisiana State University Press, 1972), 26.
2. Chulwon Cho, *The literary Tensions in Stephen Crane's Novels and Short Stories* (Seoul: American Studies Institute, Seoul National University, 1999), 21.

CHAPTER 2. MAGGIE'S WORLD

1. *The Collected Letters of Joseph Conrad*, ed. Frederick R. Karl and Laurence Davies, 5 vols. to date (Cambridge: Cambridge University Press, 1983), vol. 1, 416.
2. Eric Solomon, *Stephen Crane, from Parody to Realism* (Cambridge, MA: Harvard University Press, 1966), 60, 66.

CHAPTER 3. *BLACK RIDERS*

1. Christopher Benfey, *The Double Life of Stephen Crane* (New York: Knopf, 1992), 137.
2. *Bookman*, 3 (1896), 1.

CHAPTER 4. IMAGE AND EMBLEM IN *THE RED BADGE OF COURAGE*

1. Brian Winston, 'Fumbling in the Dark', *Sight and Sound*, February 2001, 11.
2. Nigel Andrews, 'Faced with the Horror of War: Rereadings', *Financial Times*, 6 September 1997.

3. Edwin H. Cady, *Stephen Crane* (New York: Twayne, 1962), 120.
4. Kermit Vanderbilt and Daniel Weiss, 'From Rifleman to Flag-bearer: Henry Fleming's Separate Peace in *The Red Badge of Courage*', *Modern Fiction Studies*, 11 (Winter 1965/66), 378.

CHAPTER 5. LOVE, ART, WORK: *THE THIRD VIOLET*

1. John Berryman, *Stephen Crane* (New York: Sloane, 1950), 185.
2. William Andrews, 'Art and Success: Another Look at Stephen Crane's *The Third Violet*', *Wiscana Review*, 13 (1978), 71–82.

CHAPTER 6. WAR DISPATCHES

1. Michael Robertson, *Stephen Crane, Journalism, and the Making of Modern American Literature* (New York: Columbia Unniversity Press, 1997), 147.

CHAPTER 7. POINT OF VIEW AND THE SHORT STORY

1. *The Collected Letters of Joseph Conrad*, ed. Frederick R. Karl and Laurence Davies (Cambridge: Cambridge Uni ersity Press, 1983), vol. 1, 415.

CONCLUSION

1. *The Collected Letters of Joseph Conrad*, ed. Frederick R. Karl and Laurence Davies, (Cambridge: Cambridge University Press, 1983), vol. 5, 546–7.
2. Stephen Crane, *The Red Badge of Courage and Other Stories*, ed. Daniel Hoffman (New York: Harper, 1957), xix–xx.
3. Ibid., 186.
4. Ibid., 189.
5. Hershel Parker, *Flawed Texts and Verbal Icons: Literary Authority and American Fiction* (Evanston: Noarthwestern University Press, 1984), 177.

Select Bibliography

WORKS BY STEPHEN CRANE

Collected Editions

Prose and Poetry, ed. J. C. Levenson (New York: Library of America, 1984). The fullest one-volume collection of Crane's writings, this edition, except for *Maggie*, takes its texts from the Virginia Edition.

The Work of Stephen Crane, ed. Wilson Follett, 12 vols. (New York: Knopf, 1925). Though this edition of Crane's writings has been superseded, the introductions to the individual volumes, written by many of the day's finest American authors – Sherwood Anderson, Willa Cather, Joseph Hergesheimer, Amy Lowell, H. L. Mencken, Carl Van Doren – remain valuable as critical appreciations.

The University of Virginia Edition of the Works of Stephen Crane, ed. Fredson Bowers, 10 vols. (Charlottesville: University Press of Virginia, 1969–76). The most substantial collection of Crane's writings, the Virginia Edition is nevertheless problematic. Edited according to principles for establishing eclectic texts, the Virginia Edition presents texts of several works that combine features from different versions that sometimes fail to represent Crane's intentions.

First Editions

Maggie: A Girl of the Streets (A Story of New York) (New York: for the author, 1893).

The Black Riders and Other Lines (Boston: Copeland and Day, 1895).

The Red Badge of Courage: An Episode of the American Civil War (New York: D. Appleton, 1895).

George's Mother (New York and London: Edward Arnold, 1896).

The Little Regiment and Other Episodes of the American Civil War (New York: D. Appleton, 1896).
The Third Violet (New York: D. Appleton, 1897).
The Open Boat and Other Tales of Adventure (New York: Doubleday & McClure, 1898).
The Open Boat and Other Stories (London: Heinemann, 1898).
War Is Kind (New York: Frederick A. Stokes, 1899).
Active Service: A Novel. (New York: Frederick A. Stokes, 1899).
The Monster and Other Stories (New York and London: Harper, 1899).
Whilomville Stories (New York and London: Harper, 1900).
Wounds in the Rain: A Collection of Stories Relating to the Spanish–American War of 1898 (London: Methuen, 1900).
Wounds in the Rain: War Stories (New York: Frederick A. Stokes, 1900).
Great Battles of the World (Philadelphia: J. B. Lippincott, 1901).
Last Words (London: Digby, Long, 1902).
The O'Ruddy: A Romance (New York: Frederick A. Stokes, 1903).

Selected Modern Editions of Separate Works

The Correspondence of Stephen Crane, ed. Stanley Wertheim and Paul Sorrentino, 2 vols. (New York: Columbia University Press, 1988). This, the standard edition of Crane's letters, is the first to cast doubt on the surreptitious letters that appeared in Thomas Beer's *Stephen Crane*.
Maggie: A Girl of the Streets (A Story of New York), ed. Kevin J. Hayes (Boston: Bedford/St Martin's, 1999). This critical edition of the 1893 text of *Maggie* also includes numerous additional documents situating the novel within its cultural milieu.
The Notebook of Stephen Crane, ed. Donald J. Greiner and Ellen B. Greiner (Charlottesville: Bibliographical Society of the University of Virginia, 1969). A handsomely printed edition of a notebook Crane kept when he lived in New York, 1892–1894, this work is especially useful for studying his compositional process.
The Red Badge of Courage: An Episode of the American Civil War, ed. Henry Binder (1982; repr. New York: Norton, 1999). Reconstructed from Crane's surviving manuscript, Binder's text is now considered the standard edition.
The Red Badge of Courage and Other Stories, ed. Daniel Hoffman (New York: Harper, 1957). Hoffman's introduction presents a fine critical appreciation of Crane. The edition itself functions as a cultural artefact, showing how Crane's ironic war novel was repackaged for consumption after World War II.

BIBLIOGRAPHY AND REFERENCE

Dooley, Patrick K., *Stephen Crane: An Annotated Bibliography of Secondary Scholarship* (New York: G. K. Hall, 1992). Dooley has divided this work into separate sections treating biography, general criticism, and criticism directed toward individual works or groups of related works. Dooley makes no pretence toward completion and deliberately excludes book reviews.

Kibler, James E., Jr, 'The Library of Stephen and Cora Crane', *Proof*, 1 (1971), 199–246. Kibler catalogues books known to have been formerly in Crane's possession and, in so doing, provides a good starting point for those interested in studying Crane's literary influences.

Schaefer, Michael W., *A Reader's Guide to the Short Stories of Stephen Crane* (New York: G. K. Hall, 1996). Schaefer devotes individual chapters to each of Crane's short stories, all of which are similarly organized and treat the following topics: publication history, composition, sources and influences, relationships to other Crane works, and previous critical treatments.

Stallman, R. W., *Stephen Crane: A Critical Bibliography* (Ames: Iowa State University Press, 1972). Stallman's lengthy list of writings about Crane is marred by his self-serving annotations, which elevate his own work and vindictively attack those who disagree with him.

Wertheim, Stanley, *A Stephen Crane Encyclopedia* (Westport, CT: Greenwood Press, 1997). A detailed alphabetical listing of topics, from people Crane knew to characters he created, this reference work is useful for anyone studying his life and work.

BIOGRAPHY

Beer, Thomas, *Stephen Crane: A Study in American Letters* (New York: Knopf, 1923). The first book-length Crane biography, Beer's work is now thoroughly discredited. Not only did he fabricate letters supposedly written by Crane and his correspondents, he also invented many of the details he presents as fact. Beer's literary chicanery influenced Crane biography and criticism for decades.

Benfey, Christopher, *The Double Life of Stephen Crane* (New York: Knopf, 1992). Benfey's thesis-driven study, the first biography written since Beer's fabrications have come to light, elaborates Willa Cather's idea that Crane lived a double life, first writing about subjects that interested him and then attempting to live out what he had written.

Berryman, John, *Stephen Crane* (New York: Sloane, 1950). Though Berryman's biographical information, drawn largely from Beer, is untrustworthy, his critical insight into Crane's writings remains worthy of consideration. Despite his personal reputation as a poet, Berryman is better when discussing Crane's fiction than his poetry.

Colvert, James B., *Stephen Crane* (San Diego: Harcourt Brace Jovanovich, 1984). A popular and profusely illustrated biography, this is an enjoyable, if largely uncritical, life of Crane.

Davis, Linda H., *Badge of Courage: The Life of Stephen Crane* (Boston: Houghton Mifflin, 1998). The fullest narrative biography since Stallman's *Stephen Crane,* Davis's work is generally competent though it contains little new information.

Stallman, R. W., *Stephen Crane: A Biography* (New York: G. Braziller, 1968). Valuable for the new information it contained when first published, this work has been largely superseded. Without question, Stallman's biography reveals both his fondness of Crane and his dedication to his subject, yet, as in his critical bibliography, a spirit of meanness pervades this biography.

Wertheim, Stanley, and Paul Sorrentino, *The Crane Log: A Documentary Life of Stephen Crane, 1871–1900* (New York: G. K. Hall, 1994). Though a documentary compilation rather than a narrative, *The Crane Log* may nevertheless be the finest biography of Crane available. Through excerpts of Crane's writing, contemporary reviews, letters and diary entries from friends and family, newspaper articles, and photographs, Wertheim and Sorrentino bring alive Crane's life.

CRITICISM

Andrews, William L., 'Art and Success: Another Look at Stephen Crane's *The Third Violet*', *Wascana Review,* 13 (1978), 71–82. A groundbreaking work that initiated the recognition of *The Third Violet,* which formerly had been considered little more than a potboiler, this essay first emphasized the importance of studying the novel as a story about artistic endeavour.

Bassan, Maurice (ed.), *Stephen Crane: A Collection of Critical Essays* (Englewood Cliff, NJ: Prentice-Hall, 1967). Subdivided into three sections, Bassan's collection contains reminiscences of Crane; general discussions of his works by such authors as Philip Young, Sergio Perosa, and James B. Colvert; and treatments of individual works including multiple essays on *Maggie, Red Badge,* and the short stories.

Brown, Bill, *The Material Unconscious: American Amusement, Stephen Crane and the Economies of Play* (Cambridge, MA: Harvard University Press, 1996). Brown chose an intriguing topic to study, yet this work is so overladen with obtuse critical jargon that it is virtually unreadable. It is best used as a kind of sourcebook for information regarding popular culture in Crane's day.

Cady, Edwin H., *Stephen Crane* (New York: Twayne, 1962). Cady's study represents a perspective that exemplifies the now largely outmoded approach to literary explication known as the New Criticism.

Cather, Willa, *Stories, Poems, and Other Writings*, ed. Sharon O'Brien (New York: Library of America, 1992). This collection includes Cather's disparaging reviews of *War Is Kind* and *Active Service* (pp. 913–19) and her appreciative essay, 'When I Knew Stephen Crane' (pp. 932–8).

Cho, Chulwon, *The Literary Tensions in Stephen Crane's Novels and Short Stories* (Seoul: American Studies Institute, Seoul National University, 1999). Cho argues that Crane's finest works sustain a tension between determinism and morality. After discussing the Sullivan County sketches and seeing them as largely ineffectual apprentice work, Cho devotes the remainder of the book, which is largely a synthesis of earlier scholarship, to Crane's major novels and stories.

Conrad, Joseph, *The Collected Letters of Joseph Conrad*, ed. Frederick R. Karl and Laurence Davies, 5 vols. to date (Cambridge: Cambridge University Press, 1983–). This collection contains Conrad's friendly and appreciative letters to Crane, letters to other correspondents expressing his interest in Crane's work, and letters written after Crane's death memorializing him and recognizing his accomplishment.

Gullason, Thomas A., *Stephen Crane's Career: Perspectives and Evaluations* (New York: New York University Press, 1972). Gullason collects numerous important critical essays treating several aspects of Crane's writings, and also includes a variety of other documents pertaining to Crane biography.

Halliburton, David, *The Color of the Sky: A Study of Stephen Crane* (Cambridge: Cambridge University Press, 1989). Halliburton presents freewheeling, verbose, and idiosyncratic reflections on Crane's works, touching upon subjects from folklore to phenomenology. This hit-or-miss study, though frustrating, is often insightful. Happily, his detailed index makes it easy to dip into the text.

Hayes, Kevin J., 'How Stephen Crane Shaped Henry Fleming', *Studies in the Novel*, 22 (Fall 1990), 296–307. The author studies the surviving fragments of the first draft of *The Red Badge of Courage* as a means of analysing the genesis of the novel.

Hoffman, Daniel, *The Poetry of Stephen Crane* (New York: Columbia University Press, 1956). Now approaching its half-century mark, Hoffman's study remains the fullest critical appreciation of Crane's poetry. Hoffman not only situates Crane's verse into the history of American poetry, he also examines its relationship to other discursive genres such as fables and biblical verse.

Holton, Milne, *Cylinder of Vision: The Fiction and Journalistic Writing of Stephen Crane* (Baton Rouge: Louisiana State University Press, 1972). Holton presents a sensitive and finely written critical appreciation of Crane's prose.

McGann, Jerome, *Black Riders: The Visible Language of Modernism* (Princeton: Princeton University Press, 1993). Taking his title from Crane's first collection of verse, McGann emphasizes how the appearance of the printed word has influenced the development and interpretation of modern poetry.

Mariani, Giorgio, *Spectacular Narratives: Representations of Class and War in Stephen Crane and the American 1890s* (New York: Peter Lang, 1992). Applying the thought of Fredric Jameson, among others, Mariani devotes two chapters to Crane, looking at *Maggie* and other New York city sketches in one and Crane's war fiction and reportage in the other.

Mitchell, Lee Clark (ed.), *New Essays on The Red Badge of Courage* (Cambridge: Cambridge University Press, 1986). The fullest reassessment of *Red Badge* published since the appearance of the Binder edition, Mitchell's collection includes essays by Christine Brooke-Rose, Andrew Delbanco, Howard C. Horsford, Amy Kaplan, and Hershel Parker.

Monteiro, George, *Stephen Crane's Blue Badge of Courage* (Baton Rouge: Louisiana State University Press, 2000). Having unearthed much new information from contemporary newspapers, Monteiro situates Crane's writings within the discourse of the temperance movement, showing that the links between Crane's work and temperance literature are much more pervasive than has yet been recognized.

Nagel, James, 'The American Short-Story Cycle and Stephen Crane's Tales of Whilomville', *American Literary Realism*, 32:1 (1999), 35–42. Nagel situates Crane's Whilomville stories within the genre of the short-story cycle. Though Crane did not live to publish a collection of the Whilomville tales, Nagel persuasively argues that taken together they do form a coherent whole.

——, *Stephen Crane and Literary Impressionism* (University Park: Pennsylvania State University Press, 1980). Since Joseph Conrad identified Crane as a literary impressionist, the label has often been applied to him yet seldom explained. Nagel meticulously elaborates on the meaning of literary impressionism and how Crane's work exemplifies this discursive style.

Parker, Hershel, *Flawed Texts and Verbal Icons: Literary Authority and American Fiction* (Evanston: Northwestern University Press, 1984). Chapter 6, 'The Private History of a Campaign that – Succeeded?' provides an insider's narrative of the making of the Binder edition.

Robertson, Michael, *Stephen Crane, Journalism, and the Making of Modern American Literature* (New York: Columbia University Press, 1997). Robertson first situates Crane's attitude toward journalism within the context of the times. Unlike Howells and James, who disdained newspaper articles as something well below the novel, Crane recognized the literary potential of the newspaper sketch and exploited it to his advantage. Subsequent chapters treat Crane's newspaper work in roughly chronological order, showing how Crane's journalism anticipated literary modernism.

Solomon, Eric, *Stephen Crane, from Parody to Realism* (Cambridge: Harvard University Press, 1966). This, one of the earliest detailed studies of Crane's fiction, remains one of the best. Solomon's thesis-driven work posits that Crane began by parodying contemporary forms of popular literature and argues that his unique vision allowed him to transcend parody to create stirring works that embodied his poignantly realistic vision.

Sorrentino, Paul, 'Stephen Crane's Struggle with Romance in *The Third Violet*', *American Literature*, 70 (1998), 265–91. The fullest critical study of *The Third Violet* yet, this essay situates the work within its cultural milieu. Besides examining the novel's place in the romanticism/realism conflict, Sorrentino also links it with other forms of expression including commercial art and opera.

Vanderbilt, Kermit, and Daniel Weiss, 'From Rifleman to Flagbearer: Henry Fleming's Separate Peace in *The Red Badge of Courage*', *Modern Fiction Studies*, 11 (Winter 1965/66), 371–80. A groundbreaking work, this essay was the first to recognize how Henry Fleming came to rely on the emblems of battle as a means of coping with its dangers.

Weatherford, Richard M. (ed.), *Stephen Crane: The Critical Heritage* (London: Routledge and Kegan Paul, 1973). This, the fullest collection of contemporary reviews of Crane's novels, collections of short stories, and books of verse, also contains a number of early-twentieth-century critical appreciations, too. Weatherford's collections is essential for any detailed understanding of Crane's work.

Wertheim, Stanley, and Paul Sorrentino, 'Thomas Beer: The Clay Feet of Stephen Crane Biography', *American Literary Realism*, 22:3 (1990), 2–16. Wertheim and Sorrentino reveal the extent of Thomas Beer's fabrications in his biography of Crane.

Index